It's Not the Dogs, It's the People!

A Dog Trainer's Guide to Training Humans

Nicole Wilde

It's Not the Dogs, It's the People!
by Nicole Wilde

Published by:
Phantom Publishing
P.O. Box 2814
Santa Clarita, CA 91386

First Edition
Fourth printing

Cover illustration: Jack L. McDonald

ISBN 0-9667726-3-6

*To C.C., who has stood by me
through thick and thin,
and boatloads of dog hair.*

Other books by the author:

Living with Wolfdogs

Wolfdogs A-Z: Behavior, Training & More

So You Want to be a Dog Trainer

One on One: A Dog Trainer's Guide to Private Lessons

Help for Your Fearful Dog

Getting a Grip on Aggression Cases

Energy Healing for Dogs

Don't Leave Me

Hit by a Flying Wolf

ACKNOWLEDGEMENTS

I would like to thank:

Laura Bourhenne for proofreading, suggestions and for catching those inconsistencies no one else does. A mind like a steel trap, I tell ya!

Trisha McConnell for taking time from her extremely busy schedule to review the manuscript—and for the kind words.

Paul Owens for review and comments, and for ceaslessly promoting a non-violent approach to training. You are a true light in this world.

Terry Ryan, one of the nicest, down-to-earth people I have ever met. And one of the busiest! Thanks for taking the time to review the manuscript and for your support.

Daniel Terry, my father, for proofreading and suggestions. Apparently the good grammar genes skipped a generation! Thanks to you and Mom as always for your continued love and support.

C.C., my kind, patient husband, for dutifully reading all my manuscripts and laughing in all the right places. After fifteen years together, I still say you are the best!

Last but not least, thanks to Mojo and Soko for lying by my feet listening to me swear when I get frustrated, making that silly happy face when I'm relaxed, and reminding me that when life gets too intense, it's best to drop everything and go play ball.

Table of Contents

*"We would not have careers as dog trainers
if they did not have human owners.
We save dogs one human at a time."*

- Janet Smith, Trainer and
Shelter Behavior Program Specialist

Introduction

The phone rings. A frantic voice says, "You've got to help me. (pant, pant) My name is Buddy. I can't stop jumping on people. Kids fall down when we play. Worst of all..." (the voice drops to a conspiratorial whisper) "...I heard Mom and Dad talking and I think I might be something called—high-purr!" Too bad this phone call will never happen. In the best of all worlds, dogs would tell us their problems directly and we would help solve them. Unfortunately, dogs aren't the ones calling us for help.

Ask any trainer who is harder to train, dogs or people, and you'll get a vote for the two-legged. Many dog trainers get into the profession as a natural outgrowth of their love of dogs. Many, myself included, have a great deal of patience even when training the least tractable canines. In fact, when working with a client's dog, I often hear comments like, "You're so patient!" Although I want to blurt, "Hah! You should see me in traffic!" when it comes to training, they're right. When I am centered, zen-like, in that Cosmic Training Zone, I have infinite patience. I am the person I want to be in real life. Inter-species communication flows as dog and trainer perform an intricate dance of body language and understanding. Do I have that same patience with people? ...I try.

Many trainers enjoy working with both dogs and humans. Luckily, most people we meet are a pleasure to work with, as are their dogs. But sometimes, even though we understand and accept the canine learning curve, we get frustrated and even annoyed with the human half of the equation. Let's face it, we're human too and for each of us, there are certain personality types and issues that push our buttons. No matter how calm one normally is or how pleasant training can be, there will inevitably be personal

1

challenges for any trainer who deals with human students.

When owners call for help with their dog, they have reached the point where they can no longer handle the dog's problems on their own. They might feel frustrated, angry or helpless. They might even believe the problem is somehow their own fault. Cases involving serious issues such as aggression can be particularly painful for owners on an emotional level. When you are on the receiving end of that plea for help, the way you respond can have a huge effect not only on the way the person feels, but on whether that dog will ultimately get the help he needs.

Imagine telling someone who already feels badly, "Did you really think jerking Buddy when he lunged at other dogs was a good idea? No wonder he's gotten worse!" Contrast that with, "I understand this is upsetting for you. The good news is, you've already taken the first step by calling for help and based on what you've told me, it sounds as though the situation is workable." The first response is likely to make the client feel more guilty and hopeless, while the second offers hope and support.

Although a degree or background in psychology or social work is helpful, neither is essential to being able to deal with clients effectively. Many trainers are naturally intuitive with people. Even if you are not, you can improve your skills at working with humans, just as you do with dogs. After all, as dog trainers, we are natural observers of behavior. We constantly monitor a dog's body language, gauge stress levels and adjust programs accordingly. We set dogs up to succeed by implementing proven training principles and customizing programs for each particular dog. There is no reason we can't apply those same skills and techniques to our human students.

There is obviously much more to the art of dealing with people effectively than could be covered in one book. In addition to presenting a basic groundwork, I have focused on those subjects most important to us as trainers, including difficult personality types, common "sticky situations" and the dynamics of working with children and families. There are stories and composites of stories from my own experience sprinkled throughout. Some offer suggestions on what to do, while others are examples of what *not* to do. I'll admit, I have learned a lot the hard way. It is to our benefit to regard each training interaction with a canine or human as a potential learning experience—for them and for us.

Whether you do private one-on-one training or group classes, I hope you will find this book both entertaining and helpful in your own dog training...er, people training career.

*"Coming together is beginning.
Keeping together is progress.
Working together is success."*

- Henry Ford

Pleased to Meet You

Imagine someone you've never met before is coming to your home. This stranger will be judging your dog's intelligence and behavior, as well as *your* intelligence and behavior. They might even take note of your housekeeping skills—or lack thereof. And by the way, you'll be expected to learn a new skill and practice it for the first time in front of this stranger. Do you feel apprehensive? It might seem silly to you, but that's just how many clients feel when a trainer comes to their home for the first time.

When someone calls a trainer, it is an admission of needing professional help. That alone can cause some owners emotional distress. Then there are those who have had a bad experience with a previous trainer or with training in general. Some owners are afraid of looking inept or answering questions incorrectly, while others worry their dog will do something embarrassing. For everyone's sake, let's put clients at ease. Just as we wouldn't jump into working with a dog without an initial greeting and a short getting-to-know-you session, we shouldn't start firing off questions at clients without first establishing rapport.

First Impressions

Rapport begins with first impressions. Your client's first impression of you should be one of friendliness and professionalism. Arrive on time, dressed appropriately. A clean t-shirt and jeans without holes or tears is fine. A t-shirt or polo shirt emblazoned with your company logo is even better. You should appear clean, fresh and ready for work. (That applies whether you do in-home training or group classes.) When the door opens, look directly into the person's eyes, smile and shake his or her hand firmly while saying, "Hi _____, nice to meet you. I'm _____." If the dog is present and appears nervous or aggressive, explain why you are not offering to shake the client's hand.

Funny, I Feel So Relaxed...

Dogs absorb less information and learn less efficiently when they are stressed. The same applies to people. It is crucial not only to establish rapport, but to help clients feel relaxed. This will help them to understand and retain information, and will improve our chances of getting candid responses to questions.

Since we each have a unique personality, how we put clients at ease will vary. I often use humor. If Mary apologizes for the mess as I walk in, I might reply, "Ah, you should see my place—it makes yours look like *Better Homes & Gardens*!" If Dave apologizes for Goldie's exuberant greeting, something along the lines of, "Aww, Goldie's just reminding me of what we need to work on. Thanks, Goldie!" should elicit a smile. Forced humor won't help anyone, but if it comes naturally, use it.

"What a Lovely Porcelain Porcupine!"

Offering a compliment is another way to put clients at ease. I often find myself in a setting where it is no stretch to exclaim, "Your home is beautiful!" Or perhaps the blouse the client is wearing is worthy of comment. (Be careful about comments regarding physical appearance if you are a male trainer working with a female client, so as not to put her on the defensive.) Don't be insincere, but do let people know there is *something* you like about them, their house or their dog. Given that most dog trainers love dogs, it shouldn't be hard to find something complimentary to say about Goldie.

A compliment lets the client know you approve of something from the get-go. It also puts you on the same team and helps the person to relax. After greeting a particularly adorable, wriggling bundle of fur, I might smile at the client and say, "Ah, I see the problem. Your puppy is obviously suffering from excessive cuteness!" Or perhaps a breed-specific comment is in order: "It's unfortunate that Pit Bulls get such a bad rap. They are such a stable, affectionate breed." Again, make the comment only if you are sincere.

Maintaining Rapport

Once established, maintaining rapport from session to session is important. Clients should always feel that you listen and that you care. Perhaps at the last session they mentioned little Suzy was not feeling well, or that Bobby was studying for an important exam. Maybe the family was going on vacation, or Mom was having surgery. Whatever it was, if it's not too personal, inquire about it at the next session. How was the vacation? Is Suzy feeling better? How did Bobby's test go? If, like me, you would never remember these personal details, jot them down on the client's personal information sheet or wherever you keep session notes. Giving this type of personal attention makes clients feel you care; and you should. Maintining a good rapport will help to ensure continued compliance and success in the training process.

7

"When people talk, listen completely.
Most people never listen."

- Ernest Hemingway

"The only thing that is sure to keep you from
finding the truth is to believe you already have it."

- Chuck Missler

History 101

Setting the Stage

It is important that clients remain relaxed and focused as you take a history. To that end, minimize distractions as much as possible. Suggest letting the answering machine pick up calls. If the television is on, ask that it be turned off. If it looks as though your client might not be adept at redirecting young kids from being rowdy or interrupting, suggest they watch a video in another room, play a game or do homework while you chat. You could even bring along connect-the-dots pages or coloring sheets to keep them busy.

If kids are at an age where they can participate and answer questions, great. Let them stay. They might have valuable input and should be part of the training process if they are interested. Besides, every trainer has had that "kids say the darndest things" moment, where the child blurts out some key bit of information Mom or Dad never would have offered!

Some trainers prefer the dog be present during the history-taking process, as valuable information can be gleaned by observing interactions between dog and owner during this time. Another advantage is the opportunity to surreptitiously evaluate the dog's behavior while he is presumably being ignored.

If the dog is too much of a distraction to you or the owner, have him elsewhere while you chat. Some trainers prefer this arrangement not only because it minimizes distractions, but because some owners feel inhibited talking about their dog's problems with the dog present. Imagine you are taking a history

9

on a dog who has bitten someone—an emotionally loaded issue for any owner. You might not get all the honest details if the dog is lying curled up at the owner's feet, looking adorable.

Can You Hear Me Now?

Taking an effective history involves the art of listening. Pay attention as your client speaks. Do not let your attention wander— you might miss a crucial piece of information. Encourage clients to open up by showing that you are listening. Lean slightly forward and focus on the speaker, nodding your head and murmuring a soft, "Mmm-hmm" where appropriate. Do not interrupt! If the client mentions something you would like to question further or prompts you to think of a possible solution, jot it down so you can come back to it when the person has finished speaking.

It is extremely important not to appear judgmental when listening to clients. Even if you are appalled at what someone is saying, refrain from looking so, or worse, voicing your disapproval. If I have asked what someone has tried so far to stop a barking problem and the person replies, "He wears a shock collar twenty-four hours a day," regardless of the fact that I do not use nor do I approve of shock collars, I will not jump down the person's throat. Instead, I'll say lightly, "I'll make some suggestions later on about other methods that might be more productive" and move on.

No matter how atrocious a thing someone tells you (and we've all heard some truly awful things), you must put on a poker face. If the client feels you disapprove or dislike them, you are not likely to get truthful responses. I have had countless clients who, when asked where the dog sleeps, practically cringe as they answer, "On the bed?" It's as though they expect to be reprimanded. They are so relieved when I laugh and tell them it's

10

okay, I'm not going to say the dog can't sleep on the bed. (Of course, if there is a dominance-aggression issue or other reason the dog should not sleep on the bed I will say so.) To take a thorough history is to be on a fact-finding mission, nothing more. Remain neutral, alleviate apprehensions and help your clients to relax and open up.

Is That Your Final Answer?

Sometimes getting useful information requires a bit of detective work. Let's say you have inquired about the dog's reaction to other dogs on walks and the client has responded, "He just goes nuts." Do you arch an eyebrow, mutter a meaningful "hmm" and scribble "Just goes nuts"? Of course not. You ask the client to define specifically what that means. "Goes nuts" could, after all, mean "wags his tail happily and tries to get to other dogs to play" to one person, while it means "lunges, snarls and tries to hurt other dogs" to another.

Don't settle for generalities. "He gets plenty of exercise" could mean the dog spends his days alone in the yard, and the owner thinks the dog entertains himself by running around out there. At that point you might ask specifically what the owner does *with* the dog for exercise. Does the dog get taken for walks? If so, how often? For how long? At what pace? Do the walks tire the dog? Does anyone throw the ball for him? Does he play with other dogs? Do the kids spend time in the yard with him? You see where this is going. You can give much better recommendations if you have specific, accurate information with which to work.

Some questions should purposely be left open-ended. For example, rather than asking, "Did Rusty seem tense or afraid when the plumber walked in?" (*Objection! Leading the witness!*) say,

11

"What was Rusty's reaction when the plumber walked in?" If the answer is a generalization such as "He seemed scared," probe further with other open-ended questions: "Can you describe what you mean by scared? What was Rusty doing that gave you that impression?" If the client still doesn't give specifics, move to asking questions that require specific answers. You could ask whether Rusty barked, cowered, or had his hackles up; was he moving toward the door or away from it; did he cringe and/or lower his body; were his ears forward or back? Your client is not likely to know all the answers, as things happen quickly and the average person is not trained to observe the minutiae of canine body language and behavior. Still, these prompts should trigger answers that offer some helpful information.

Some questions should be specific and detailed from the beginning. For example, when asking about feeding, you might ask what brand of food the dog eats, how many times a day he's fed, at what times he's fed, where he eats, whether he finishes all the food that's offered and whether the bowl is picked up afterward. Contrast the usefulness of those answers with simply learning the dog is fed dry kibble twice a day. What if the low-quality grains in that particular brand of food are affecting the dog's behavior? What if he's fed twice a day, doesn't eat right away, and the food is left there? Since the food is always available, it is less valuable. This is all pertinent information that will affect how you proceed. (Note: For a sample general intake form, see my book *So You Want to be a Dog Trainer*.)

Oh, and One More Thing…

Regardless of how thorough your questions have been, it is a good idea when wrapping up a subject to ask "Is there anything more you'd like me to know?" Incredibly helpful information can be uncovered this way. In fact, it might even contain the key to the dog's behavior problem. Even though I have asked a number of specific feeding-related questions, the "anything more" question might elicit, "Well, if Mini doesn't eat when I first put the food down, I add some gravy to it and if she still doesn't eat, I give her a few pieces of boiled chicken." This telling reply contains valuable information about the dog-owner relationship.

Although you have asked the "anything more" question at the close of each subject, it is a good idea to ask it again at the end of the entire history-taking process. Ask whether there is anything that has not been covered, that is important for you to know. Again, invaluable information can be obtained this way.

Now that you have taken a history and established rapport with your human trainee, let's move on to some actual "human training" skills!

"No matter how good your mission, no matter how sure you are of it, no matter how passionate you feel about it, you will never make it happen unless others become invested in it and are motivated to take the necessary steps."

- Kate White

"Kind words can be short and easy to speak, but their echoes are truly endless."

- Mother Teresa

Basic Human-Training Skills

Treat your Clients like Dogs

Good trainers employ sound principles, patience and consistency when working with dogs. Great trainers apply those things to both dogs and humans. After all, what we really do is train people to train their dogs. How many times have you been in a training situation where the owner suddenly laughs and exclaims, "You're really training me!" And it's true. Following are basic principles for training the two-legged contingent.

Learning Styles

> *"Tell me and I will forget. Show me and I will remember. Involve me and I will learn."*
> - Chinese Proverb

Everyone has a personal learning style. Some people like to listen to new information. Others are more visual and prefer to read or see something demonstrated. But as Volhard and Fisher state in *Teaching Dog Obedience Classes* (see *Resources*), "Research has shown that the average person accurately remembers only 10% of what he hears." Imagine what your students would retain if all you did was lecture. Can you picture giving a verbal explanation of a down-stay, then expecting your students to follow through? The authors go on to state that "adding demonstrations will increase retention to about 35%, and actually doing it, to about 50%." While there is nothing we can do to guarantee all students will understand and retain information, we can set things up to give them the best chance to succeed. Sound familiar? Human and dog training have a lot in common.

15

It's Not the Dogs, It's the People!

As we teach a new behavior, whether in a private appointment or group class, we explain what we are doing. But no matter how good your explanation or demonstration, it is no substitute for your students actually going through the motions and practicing the exercise. Let's face it, a triple axel looks easy when Nancy Kerrigan does it, but I doubt any of us could pull it off on the first try, no matter how many times we'd seen it done.

I have watched group classes and sat in on private appointments where an otherwise excellent instructor assumed owners understood instructions and could carry out an exercise without even having them try it. Regardless of how much head-nodding and "Mmm-hmm"ing is going on as you demonstrate, you must have students actually try the exercise themselves. Otherwise, there is no opportunity for you to give constructive feedback, and they or their dogs may develop bad habits. If more than one family member will be working with the dog, have each person try it so you can individualize feedback and instructions.

Break It Down

As trainer Bob Bailey says, training is a mechanical skill. We trainers have, over hundreds or thousands of repetitions, become proficient at performing precise training maneuvers. Owners often tell us, "It looks so easy when you do it!" The trick is to never forget how it felt when you were first learning.

I strongly suggest every trainer periodically learn a new skill. I recently took a belly dancing class. Who knew that moving your upper body one way as your lower body gyrates in a completely different direction is so hard! I felt more than a bit foolish, and at times, frustrated. It certainly gave me a whole new empathy for clients who are trying to juggle a clicker, leash and treats.

Just as dogs learn better when a behavior is broken down into sections, so do humans. While many of us are meticulous about splitting a behavior into tiny increments so a dog can succeed, we ignore the human learning curve. Let's make it easy for our students. When Anna is having trouble managing the timing of the click and dispensing Roxy's treats while holding the leash, don't stand there and watch her struggle. Suggest she hold the leash and concentrate on the timing of the click; you dispense the treats. Do this until she gets the hang of it and can handle it all on her own. When Dan attempts to put a Gentle Leader on Rudy for the first time, break it down. First, have him get comfortable with putting the muzzle loop on. Then add the fastening of the straps around the head. We must instill confidence in our clients, which will happen naturally if we give them small tasks that are easily accomplished.

I recently had a client I'll call Rhonda. We were teaching her German Shepherd, Hannah, to respond to verbal cues to stop in her tracks and return to Rhonda regardless of what was going on in the environment. (We had already trained Hannah to "Wait" and "Come".) The exercise began with Rhonda holding a long line and allowing Hannah to wander a short distance away. She would then say, "Wait" in a firm voice. When Hannah froze, Rhonda would immediately call, "Hannah, come!" in a happy, enthusiastic voice, and Hannah would run to her. We went over the instructions carefully, I demonstrated a few times, and Rhonda said she understood.

The first time Rhonda tried it, she let Hannah out a bit, then said, "Hannah, wait!" I reminded her of the verbal sequence. The second time she did the same thing, but caught her mistake. Another two repetitions proved that although she realized what she was doing wrong, Rhonda couldn't seem to get the words out correctly. At least she was laughing, and I laughed along with her. (It's fine to laugh *with* your clients—laughing relieves tension—just don't laugh *at* them.) At that point, simply explaining it again would not have been sufficient, so we broke it down. I asked Rhonda if I could take Hannah's leash. By the way, it is rude to snatch a leash from a client's hands. Always ask permission. (Sometimes I will put my hand out toward the leash and say, "May I have this dance?" When handing the dog back I will sometimes say, "Your witness." What can I tell you, I'm silly. But better silly than rude.)

Getting back to Rhonda...I held the long line and let Hannah wander a few feet away from Rhonda, with no distractions present. I then asked Rhonda to call Hannah to her. "Hannah, come!" she called. Hannah flew to her. Perfect! We repeated this a few times. Then I handed Rhonda the long line and told her all I wanted her to focus on was the "Wait". When Hannah got a few feet away, Rhonda yelled, "Wait". I immediately said, "Now call her" and Rhonda did, getting it exactly right. In subsequent repetitions, she did the entire sequence flawlessly. Success!

It is inevitable that no matter how good an instructor you are, some clients will still get frustrated when trying to learn something new. I often remind clients that when they first started driving, it seemed there were endless things to remember and coordinate. Eventually, everything gelled into one fluent operation. Physical repetition leads to muscle memory, so movements become fluid without conscious effort. Mental sequences become automatic.

Continually assess your clients' skill levels and observe their movements as you would a dog's. Keep adjusting your program accordingly, and be patient. Just as we do not expect a dog to get something right the first time, we should not expect immediate success from our clients.

Positive Reinforcement

As trainers who rely heavily on positive reinforcement, we understand the need to reward a dog for a job well done. But how many of us apply that same principle to people? How many "jackpot" a client for a "Breakthrough Performance on a Training Exercise"? (There ought to be an award for that category, don't you think?) A big smile along with an enthusiastic, "Yes! That's it! You've got it!" can make a client feel every bit as reinforced as a dog receiving a shower of hot dogs.

Some people need more reassurance than others. But everyone, regardless of his confidence level, wants to hear he is doing well. I learned that lesson long before I ever became a dog trainer. The first job I ever held was as an instructor at a health spa. This was in my teenage years, back when jeans were still called dungarees and aerobics was called calisthenics. (Okay, I'm ancient.) My duties included leading women through their exercises, showing them how to use the equipment, and offering feedback and support.

I have never forgotten what we instructors were told to do if a member did an exercise incorrectly. We were never to "correct" the woman, but instead, to frame suggestions in a positive light. Instead of snapping, "That's wrong, Dolores!" we'd offer, "Very good, Dolores! Now, the next time, let's try bringing the bar down a bit slower." That lesson stuck with me. Not only did the "let's try" frame things in a positive way, it made the person feel we were in this together, and together we'd find a solution.

By contrast, my first experience assisting a trainer in group classes was quite different. As a fledgling trainer, I was anxious to apprentice with an experienced one. A man I knew who bred the type of dogs I was involved in rescuing at the time, also offered group classes. I ended up driving two hours every Saturday to assist in his group that began at 7:30 a.m. Unfortunately, this trainer used harsh corrections with both dogs and people. I got yelled at constantly. Apparently, I had an abhorrent habit of patting or talking to the dogs now and then as I worked them. "Wilde, dammit," he'd bellow for all to hear, "Stop coddling that dog!" To this day I can't bring myself to use the word "coddle".

There was harsh criticism of footwork, timing, technique and more, all quite loudly and publicly. I admit there was even a time or two I found myself in tears. And it wasn't just me. The more the instructor yelled at and berated his students, the more stressed they got and the worse they performed; which, of course, led to even harsher verbal corrections. I took the verbal abuse as best I could. But the day I saw him hang an eight week old puppy from a choke chain, I left. I learned a lot from the experience. Mostly, I learned what methods I did *not* want to use with dogs or people, and about the fallout aversives can create.

It is our job as trainers, no matter how inept a student might be, to remain cool and encouraging. After all, the student is probably frustrated enough for both of us. Find *something* the person is doing right and comment on it. *Then* make suggestions for improvement. For example, "Your praise voice is excellent, and I love the animation you put into this. Now let's work on the timing of the click." Contrast that with the effect it would have if you nodded your head sadly and sighed, "I'm sorry, but you're just not getting it. Let's move on to something else."

Be positive, but don't be insincere or overly complimentary. After all, if you constantly rave, "That was perfect!" there's nowhere to go from there to deliver a verbal "jackpot". Be specific in your praise. Rather than the general "That's better," say "Your timing was much better that time" or "That's the body posture we're looking for."

Another way to make your clients feel positively reinforced is to say something nice about their dogs. This one is easy for most trainers. Tell the client the dog is intelligent; adorable; really sweet; has a beautiful coat. It really doesn't matter, so long as it is complimentary. There are some dogs I am so crazy about, I ask permission to clone them. Whatever the compliment, you can bet the owner will feel good about it and will proudly repeat what you have said to friends and family. That sense of well-being will translate to your students relaxing, liking their trainer and their dog, and feeling good about training in general.

Keep it Real

Many dog trainers are fascinated with the minutiae of the training process. We could train dogs all day long—and often do. We can appreciate a behavior modification protocol that has sixty-seven tiny, incremental steps, and patiently observe tiny improvements in a dog's behavior as he progresses. Your average client, however, just wants the dog to stop jumping, nipping or digging—and it would be nice if the problem could be solved yesterday! Regardless of whether you are working with simple obedience or complex behavior issues, it is crucial that the protocols you suggest are realistic ones your clients are willing and able to follow.

As professional trainers, we assess situations and offer solutions based on our experience and expertise. Unfortunately, sometimes the method we know would be most effective is not workable for a particular client. That's okay. There is always Plan B. If we stubbornly insist on Plan A even though the client has clearly indicated it is not feasible, everyone loses. We must make modifications and formulate a plan that works for everyone.

I had a client once named Sheila, whose Miniature Poodle, Mimi, had a housebreaking problem. Mimi was left alone with full access to the house whenever Sheila was gone, up to three hours at a time. Sheila would return home to find that Mimi had urinated on the carpet. When I suggested crating Mimi while she was gone, a look bordering on terror crossed Sheila's face. When I started to explain what crate training was all about, she cut me off. "No," she said in a stern voice, "I won't do it. I'm not locking Mimi in that tiny box." When I suggested closing bedroom doors so Mimi wouldn't have access to the things she was destroying, I was met with another firm refusal. Sounds strange, doesn't it?

It turned out Sheila was claustrophobic, and was projecting her fears on to her dog. While Mimi might have been perfectly fine in a crate, the thought of that confined space made Sheila so uncomfortable, she just couldn't bring herself to do it. Fortunately, we were able to come up with a workable solution that included the use of tethers and some scheduling changes in Sheila's routine.

Be creative and stay flexible. Being flexible, by the way, is not to be confused with bending over backward for clients who continually challenge what you say or refuse to cooperate. We'll get to those types in a bit. Just remember, it's not what you think the client should be able to do, but what works for them that is important. Making modifications to your programs and customizing them to each client's needs is one mark of a great trainer.

Verbal Skills

You could be the most knowledgeable dog trainer in the universe, but it would be worthless if you did not also possess the ability to impart information to your clients in a way they could understand. Following are some verbal techniques that can help.

Skip the Mumbo-Jumbo and Do the Hokey Pokey

Although you might be a walking encyclopedia of learning theory, there is no need to use scientific jargon with your clients. Just as you wouldn't ask a dog to "Sit" by saying "Kindly maneuver your hindquarters so as to be flush with the floor," there is no reason to confuse your clients with verbal mumbo-jumbo. No one will be served by your spouting terms like "Premack principle" and "cognitive dissonance." After all, training should not be about impressing clients with how much *you* know, but impressing them with how well *they* can do training their dog. Be sure to explain phrases and concepts simply and clearly.

Remember that old song, the "Hokey Pokey"? *"You put your left foot in, you take your left foot out, you put your left foot in and you shake it all about…"* Silly as it is, those lyrics are a perfect example of the type of clear instructions we should be giving our clients. Saying "Lure your dog into a sit" is not specific. "Luring means getting the dog to follow something, in this case a food treat. Hold the treat in your right hand. Now, move your hand from the dog's nose…" and so on, is clear and specific. Keep instructions as straightforward and simple as possible.

It's Not the Dogs, It's the People!

I'll Say It Again...

Given that 10% retention figure, it will be necessary to repeat yourself. Whether you are teaching in a group or private setting, your students might miss what you say the first time. Vary the way you repeat instructions, but do repeat them, reiterating the most important points at the end. It is more likely that students will retain the last thing they hear. Of course, pertinent information should also be repeated on the homework sheet. That way, even if a student were preoccupied with what her dog was doing during class, she could absorb the information later when there are less distractions.

Even if you have been clear and specific and have repeated instructions, some students still might not understand. In that case, find a different way to explain things. For example, if the student still does not understand how to move the lure to get the dog from a sit into a down position, you could say, "Imagine drawing the letter L." Now the student has a clear visual to hold in mind as she lures. As trainers, we naturally switch training tactics when a dog is not getting it. We must use this same willingness to adapt the instruction to fit the pupil when training humans.

Painting with Words

Be aware of the pictures you paint with your words. Let's say Chelsea, a ten-month-old Golden Retriever, is digging up Dave's back yard. You could say, "Well, Dave, if you don't start giving Chelsea some exercise, pretty soon your back yard will look like the surface of the moon!" Sure, that lets Dave know Chelsea needs more exercise, and it's humorous to boot. But it also paints a bleak picture in Dave's mind of the destruction Chelsea could cause.

24

Contrast that with the visualization encouraged by saying, "I'll bet if you start taking Chelsea for walks twice a day and giving her lots of chew toys and attention, your yard will look beautiful again. And, Chelsea will be much more relaxed in the evenings." Paints a whole different picture, doesn't it?

Anything can be framed in a positive or negative light. Be aware of how you verbally paint scenarios, because it can have a major impact on how the client perceives the situation. Humans are, after all, similar to dogs in that we only put effort into something if we see the value in it for us. Framing things in a positive light gives clients a mental picture of what's in it for them if they comply.

The Phrase that Pays... And a Few that Don't

When working with a client, you are the expert. You should exude a quiet authority and make recommendations with confidence. However, no matter how much experience and expertise you have, recommendations should be framed as suggestions rather than orders. "Butch would really benefit from more exercise" has a softer tone than the commanding "You need to make more of an effort to give Butch exercise" or even the accusatory "You haven't been giving Butch enough exercise." The former is more likely to gain compliance, while the latter two might cause resentment and lessen the chance that your client will listen to your suggestions with an open mind.

Start sentences with phrases such as "Let's try..." or "Here's something I've found helpful" rather than "You must..." or "You should". Begin to notice the way you phrase things and if necessary, modify your approach. You might be surprised at the increase in owner compliance.

Everyone, no matter how confident, can be sensitive about certain things. It is important not to inadvertently touch upon someone's sore spots. If, for example, you feel it is important to recommend that a dog lose weight and the owner is overweight as well, phrase your suggestion carefully. "Gigi is a bit overweight. Since German Shepherds can be prone to hip dysplasia, we want to be especially careful not to stress those hip joints" is infinitely kinder than, "Gigi is really obese. All that fat pressing on her hip joints can cause problems." Don't avoid touchy subjects if they are important to cover. Just be aware of the way you phrase things.

Speaking of sensitivities, don't be "breedist". While we all have our own personal biases regarding certain breeds, it is not necessary to share your negative ones with clients. So you think Labs are obnoxious, hyperactive and not pleasant to be around. Or that German Shepherds are neurotic; or Shelties are barky. Perhaps you even call Jack Russells "Jack Russell Terrorists" in private. (Please don't shoot me. These are just examples. Really.) Does that mean you are going to share these gems with clients? No. Instead of saying, "Geez, Buddy is really hyper. I give you a lot of credit. I couldn't live with a Lab" you say, "I wish I had half of Buddy's energy." That German Shepherd isn't neurotic, it's "sensitive". You see where this is going.

Keep your breed prejudices to yourself and keep an open mind. Who knows, you might even change your tune after meeting a few particularly nice representatives of that breed. More importantly, you haven't offended your client.

Blending – It's Not Just for Margaritas, Anymore!

In *Dealing With People You Can't Stand* (see *Resources*), Dr.

26

Rick Brinkman and Dr. Rick Kirschner describe "blending," a process by which people get along better by emphasizing the similarities between them: "You blend visually with your facial expression, degree of animation, and body posture. You blend verbally with your voice volume and speed. And you blend conceptually with your words…" They go on to warn, "The failure to blend has serious consequences, because without blending the differences between you become the basis for conflict."

Blending is necessary to make people feel as though you are on their side, which is necessary to move any interaction in the direction you want it to go. In training, clients must feel you are on their side before they will accept your suggestions. Blend by being adaptive in your mannerisms and recommendations. For example, if you walk into a home filled with religious icons, you might want to watch your language more carefully than usual. If your clients seem down to earth and casual, your own mannerisms and speech pattern might take on a more relaxed tone. You can even slightly increase or decrease the speed at which you speak to better match the pace of your client's speech.

You can also blend with clients by letting them know you have had the same experiences they have. When Bob tells you he is angry that Misty chewed his favorite pair of shoes, you could admonish him to be more careful and not leave his shoes on the floor. And you'd be right. Personally, I might first tell Bob about the time I came home to find that my pup Mojo had chewed my entire CD collection, and describe how angry I was. Really? Even a trainer's dog could do something wrong? Who knew! Maybe Misty isn't so bad after all.

Clients assume trainers' dogs are perfect. They are often relieved to find out that's not true. By sharing this story I have put us on

27

the same side and we can proceed from there. Now when I suggest that Bob keep his shoes picked up, he is more likely to go along with the suggestion. Blending is a beautiful thing!

Blending can make or break a relationship. Years ago, I worked in a corporate office. The president's administrative assistant was in charge of other assistants on the floor. This woman was high-energy and extremely focused—a human Border Collie. When she asked for something to be done, it was in a crisp, no-nonsense manner that left no room for disagreement. Although I was good at my job and always produced work on time, it irked her no end when I answered her in my usual laid-back speech pattern. "Sure, no problem" could send her into a tizzy for hours. What she had wanted was a crisp, "Yes ma'am, I'll have that report to you within the hour." My natural speech pattern was misinterpreted as a lack of respect for her or the company, and it caused problems.

Blending is crucial to any working relationship, be it a corporate or canine environment. You do not need to be a chameleon, but do be aware of your client's basic personality. You probably already "blend" subconsciously with your clients to some extent, but it doesn't hurt to be more consciously aware of it.

It's Like... an Analogy

Using analogies is one of my favorite ways to get clients to understand a concept. Sure, I explain that behaviors that are rewarded are more likely to be repeated. But contrast the dryness of simply stating that, with telling clients to imagine that each time you call them over they will receive a $50 gift certificate; then asking what they think they might do the next time you call them over. Most people break into a wide grin when answering that one—and they definitely "get it".

Sure, we should explain the desensitization process and the need to manage the dog so as not to surpass the dog's threshold during the process, but I use a scorpion analogy. (Most people use spiders for this one but hey, I live in the desert, scorpions are everywhere, and they're kind of creepy.) "Let's say you're afraid of scorpions," I'd say. "You could probably handle it if, while we sat in your living room, I pointed one out to you on the far wall. You'd see the scorpion, then I would give you a piece of chocolate. Each time I visit, we would decrease the distance to the scorpion in tiny bits, always maintaining your comfort level, giving you that piece of chocolate every time. But what if, during this training process, you woke up and there was a scorpion on your pillow? Aaack! That would certainly set the process back, wouldn't it? It's the same thing with Buffy and other dogs. We need to get her used to them gradually." Analogies help to make theories understandable.

Another common analogy is helpful in convincing clients to discontinue using a training method that is not working. For example, each time Jane's Weimeraner jumps on her, she puts her knee up. She has been taught this is the right thing to do. However, when questioned as to whether it has worked, Jane sheepishly answers no. You might suggest, "You wouldn't continue to take a medication that no longer works; so why continue using a method that doesn't work?" You can almost see the light bulb go on over a clients head with that one.

Humor can be integrated into analogies. When I tell clients it might take some time for their dog to acclimate to wearing a head halter, I remind them of how uncomfortable it felt the first time they wore glasses or a brassiere, and how they eventually got used to it. Then, with my usual twisted sense of humor, I'll turn to the man in the couple and say, "You remember the first time you wore a bra, don't you?" I haven't had a single client who didn't laugh at that. Of course, you should always be aware of the personality of the person you are addressing and use humor only where appropriate.

Perhaps you already use all the aforementioned skills without even realizing it. But even if you do, pick one and concentrate on it the next time you work with a client. You might be surprised at the increased compliance and level of success. Be more conscious of what you do and say. After all, being a good trainer of humans means training ourselves as well, and modifying our approach when necessary.

Handouts Are Your Friends

There is one distinct advantage training humans has over training dogs: humans can read. Whether you do group classes or in-home training, giving pre-printed handouts is an excellent way to ensure that your students retain vital information. If you are at a private session teaching Donna to get Dusty to "leave it" but her kids keep interrupting and the phone rings repeatedly, it is not likely that Donna is going to remember much of what you have said.

Even if you have a client's undivided attention, unless the person has a photographic memory, total retention is still unlikely. (Remember that 10% figure!) In a group class setting, things can be even more hectic and distracting. Handouts fill in any information that was not absorbed or that you might have forgotten to impart. After all, you are human too and at some point will be distracted or have an off day.

The Usual Suspects

Handouts I have written and use regularly include *Leadership Program, Crate Training, Basic Principles of Positive Training, Clicker Training, How to Stuff a Kong* and *Recommended Reading*. Then there are more specialized handouts on topics such as resource guarding and introducing dogs to babies. I am forever adding and revising my handouts.

You could have separate handouts for individual behaviors you teach, programs you normally have owners follow, or information on topics you feel are important, i.e. nutrition or health. I give so many handouts, I joke with my clients they'll soon have enough to paper their walls with. The fact is, handouts are appreciated

31

and useful, and make you look professional and well organized.

Handouts don't necessarily have to be written by you. I give all my puppy owners Leslie Nelson and Gail Pivar's excellent booklet, *Taking Care of Puppy Business*. For leadership, Patricia McConnell's *Leader of the Pack* can't be beat, and her *Cautious Canine* always finds its way to clients whose dogs need desensitization and counter-conditioning. There is a ton of detail packed into those little booklets, and they can be purchased in bulk at low prices. (See *Resources* for all of the above.) Clients love getting freebies! If you feel giving these booklets away is too much of a financial burden, raise your prices a few dollars to cover the cost.

Handouts by authorities such as veterinarians can be used to support information you disseminate. You can also use copies of articles from magazines (with permission and copyright credit) and newspapers for this purpose. Sometimes seeing the information in print gives clients the push they need to follow suggestions.

Homework Sheets

Another useful type of handout is the homework sheet. These pre-printed pages can serve as reminders of what was covered during a training session, and to outline specific instructions on how to proceed between sessions.

A homework sheet should be clear, concise, and in most cases, one page. First, it should define the exercise or goal. For example, "Goal: For your dog to lie down when you give the hand signal or the verbal cue 'Down'". It should briefly review the steps to teach the dog to lie down, and the hand signal.

Next, it should offer specific suggestions on how often and in what situations to practice. For example, "Practice downs in short, three-to-five-minute sessions throughout the day." Describe real-life practice situations as well: "When your dog approaches, sits and paws to solicit petting, ask him to lie down. Once he's down, reward with attention." Or, "A great time to practice downs is during television commercials."

Compare the value of those specific written tips with the general verbal instruction to "practice the down with your dog." Finish with general tips. For example, "Practice downs when your dog is tired" or "Some dogs prefer to lie on carpeting. If yours does, make it easy by practicing in a carpeted area first."

Be sure to review handouts and homework sheets periodically and revise as needed.

"The task of the excellent teacher is to stimulate 'apparently ordinary' people to unusual effort. The tough problem is not in identifying winners: it is in making winners out of ordinary people."

- K. Patricia Cross

"Advise is like snow; the softer it falls the longer it dwells upon, and the deeper it sinks into the mind."

- Samuel Taylor Coleridge

Training Hordes of Wild Humans

Group classes present their own unique challenges. People and dogs are often nervous or excited. There are distractions. Difficult personality types crop up, both human and canine. It is impossible to concentrate your time and energy on each individual as much as you might like, regardless of how many assistants you have. You must consider the pacing of the class and how to keep people motivated so they will keep coming back for more. Though the challenges are numerous, group classes can be fun and rewarding to teach. They can also offer an excellent opportunity to train many humans at once. Here are some keys to making it all work.

Size Does Matter!

If you teach alone, you probably will not want more than six to eight students per class. That number may increase depending on how many assistants and how much available space you have. The reason for keeping classes small is to be able to give students enough personal attention. We humans appreciate it when someone takes the time to address us individually and to offer customized assistance. That would be an almost impossible feat if you were teaching twenty dog-human teams on your own.

Be sure to address your students by name. We trainers know how easy it is to remember dogs' names but forget they have humans attached. I used to address students as "Maxi's Mom" or "Buddy's Dad." While it was cute, it also depersonalized things. People want to be present and accounted for. If you cannot remember names, have your students wear name tags. Or, do what I did. I would call the roll at the beginning of each class, not just to keep track of who was there, but to remind me of who was who!

35

It's Not the Dogs, It's the People!

Be sure to give each student individual attention and feedback. You might have a favorite person you pay more attention to, or a breed that you tend to use more often for demonstrations. Or perhaps there is a breed of dog you dislike and tend to avoid. Despite your personal preferences, try to give equal attention to all. I know a woman who has a tiny Chinese Crested. She dropped out of two classes before joining mine because the trainers never, ever demonstrated with her dog. She felt slighted. You can bet I made a point of demonstrating with her dog, who by the way, was lovely and did wonderfully. The owner felt validated and continued classes.

Take It Easy

Most students are nervous the first night of a group class. They are afraid their dog will be the worst one there or do something to embarrass them. When I did puppy classes, a pup or two would invariably urinate in the classroom. The owners would be mortified. I'd laugh and tell them it was completely natural, then clean it up and get back to business. But I could imagine how embarrassed they felt. Whatever the situation, try to make students as comfortable as possible by maintaining a relaxed atmosphere.

Just as we encourage dogs to enjoy training, we must do the same for our human students. The fastest way to do this is to make them feel successful and confident. Nothing elicits a smile like an owner realizing she can actually train her dog to do something! So make it easy. Start with something simple. For example, instruct owners to play the "attention game" at the first class. Each time the dog looks at them, they are to give the dog a treat (or click and treat, if you are clicker training). Very soon, dogs will be paying attention to their very pleased owners, who will be thinking *gee, maybe this training thing isn't so hard after all.*

Keep things simple and manageable. If a student is having trouble holding the leash and treats while performing an exercise, offer to help by tethering the dog to something. If you have assistants, be sure they notice and assist those who are having trouble.

Structure Matters, Too

Another thing that will make learning easier for students is to structure the progression of your exercises wisely. Build on behaviors that have already been learned. For example, if you have already taught the dogs to sit, at the next class you could have them sit, then walk a few steps and sit again, working into loose leash walking. You wouldn't start teaching loose leash walking without the dogs ever having learned sit, since part of the exercise is for the dogs to automatically sit when the owners stop walking. Be aware of the proficiency level of your students and gear the class appropriately. Don't make things too easy, but sprinkle in easy exercises here and there to keep everyone motivated. It is fine for exercises to be somewhat challenging, but if you make them consistently too challenging, your students will lose enthusiasm.

If it appears your students are finding a new exercise too difficult, go back briefly to something they already know. Then, resume the exercise. Or, give them a break. If the dogs know how to sit, have a quick game of musical chairs or a contest to see who can do the most sits in thirty seconds. You can always break up tension by having students stop what they are doing, stand, stretch and take a few deep breaths. If more than a few students are having trouble with an exercise, review the way you are teaching it. If necessary, break it down even further into achievable parts.

It's Not the Dogs, It's the People!

"You, Over There!"

Let's say you are teaching a class where the current objective is to get the dogs to lie down on cue. You have explained and demonstrated the exercise and are now walking around coaching each student-dog team individually. While working with Debbie, you notice that over in the corner Melissa and her Bearded Collie, Winston, are having trouble. They have started the exercise with Winston in a sitting position as instructed, but Melissa keeps pulling the lure too far toward herself, rather than moving it straight down toward the ground. This causes Winston to stand up. Melissa is getting frustrated and Winston is confused. What should you do?

Since you are busy, do you shout across the room to point out what Melissa is doing wrong? No. Most likely, that would embarrass her. Ideally, you would have the time afterward to walk over and help them one-on-one or have an assistant do so. If that is not possible, once the exercise is over, address the class as a whole. "Well done!" you might say. "Now, here are a few things to keep in mind…" Then remind *all* your students to move the lure in a straight line toward the ground, along with anything else you have noticed that might improve performance. Be sure to scan the group visually as you deliver the suggestions, rather than focusing on one person.

While it is important not to single someone out for a "verbal correction," we do not normally consider it a bad idea to single someone out for praise. After all, many people would love it if we pointed them out. When you tell the class to "notice the perfect timing Lisa had in delivering the treat," Lisa might beam with pride. She might even tell her husband about it when she gets home. Lisa is self-confident, and by singling her out, you have

38

made her feel good about participating in class. Contrast that with drawing attention to a person who is painfully shy. When you say, "Class, I want you all to notice the way Sherri keeps the leash nice and loose during this exercise. Sherri, would you mind demonstrating?" Sherri just might wish she could fade into the floorboards. Unlike Lisa, Sherri does not feel better for having been singled out. She starts to suspect that joining this group, which was hard for her but she did for her dog's sake, was not such a good idea after all.

We all know a reward must be something a dog likes, or it is not a reward. The same applies to people. If you know someone well and feel confident she will appreciate being singled out publicly, go for it. If you are not sure, it is always safe to either praise the student privately or to offer praise to the group: "You guys did great on that one! You've really come a long way." Better yet, include in your praise specific things individuals did: "That time I saw relaxed arms holding leashes and good timing of treats. That's exactly what we want!"

Keep On Track

I do not know of a single group class instructor who always, without fail, sticks to lesson plans. In fact, some of the best instructors don't. It is the nature of the beast that no two groups of people, or dogs for that matter, will learn at the same rate or excel at the same things. Go with the flow of each individual class and adjust your program accordingly. That said, it is not a good idea to get so far off track that you never get to the vital exercises or information you had planned to include.

There are many personality types who can throw you off track. When Rambling Rose raises her hand to ask a question but launches into an off-topic story about her dog, you must politely but firmly cut her off and redirect the class to the topic at hand. When Look-at-Me Leah "accidentally" lets her dog get away from her for the third time, you could get irritated and point out that Leah needs to be more careful; but you'd only be calling attention to her (which is what she wants) and detracting from your teaching time. Instead, silently walk over, tether her dog to something sturdy and suggest she work that way. Then move on. Don't get sucked into heated discussions with Know-It-All Ned or Argumentative Al. Stay calm and focused, and redirect the conversation back to the task at hand. (More on these personality types and how to deal with them coming up!)

Keep It Moving

If you have ever sat through a lengthy school graduation ceremony, you can relate to that 10% retention figure. You become unfocused and lethargic, barely listening to what the speaker is saying. As an instructor, regardless of how much information you want to impart, you will be most effective if you keep your students focused. Alternate between short explanations, moving exercises and stationary ones. For example, after giving a brief explanation and then working on downs, the next exercise might be recalls, followed by down-stays. No matter how fascinating a speaker you are, your students will benefit if you keep your explanations simple and brief.

Keep It Fun

Games are a great way to keep your students motivated and enthusiastic. Never underestimate the power of fun! Play games here and there, and make sure the class atmosphere never gets too serious. Sure, you are earnest about teaching your students what they need to learn; but they should never feel tense or pressured.

Play games, laugh when appropriate (especially if *you* make a mistake), take breaks, and shower students with praise and encouragement. Students who have fun while learning are motivated students who will keep coming back for more.

"Ooh, I Want One Too!"

A great way to keep your students motivated in a group class is to positively reinforce them with *good stuff.* Some trainers award a piece of candy or a prize when someone asks an especially good question or does an exercise well. Prizes need not be big: stickers, pencils, animal-shaped erasers and other small, silly things quickly become coveted items. I know one trainer who brings a box of brightly colored, gummed stars to class; whenever a human or dog does something wonderful, the dog gets a star stuck directly on its head. It's a hoot. Her students love seeing the dogs parading around with their colorful symbols of success shining on their adorable, furry heads.

Another fun way to positively reinforce your students is to hand out Bonus Bones, a concept pioneered by trainer Terry Ryan. I printed the words Bonus Bones on card stock on the computer, then cut them out in the shape of bones. Throughout my classes, each time a person or dog did something wonderful, a Bonus Bone was awarded. At the end of the semester, students would turn in their Bonus Bones for prizes. Everyone loved it.

Be sure that regardless of what type of reward you use, that each student receives at least one during the semester. Since you can reward just about anything, i.e. perfect attendance, fastest sit, or

41

even something silly like best wagging tail, it should not be hard to find a way to reward each dog-human team.

Graduation

Be sure each class has a graduation ceremony. Just as graduation serves as a culmination of years of hard work for high school and college students, your students deserve to celebrate how far they've come. Graduating is a goal that keeps motivation high.

Be sure your ceremony includes graduation certificates (these are easy to print on the computer), prizes and plenty of fun. Graduation should not be solemn or tense. After all, you are rewarding your students for sticking with it and doing a great job. Sure, you want to be certain everyone has learned the exercises, but don't pressure anyone. Play games that use the skills they have learned. Be silly. Reward those who are most improved. Make sure all students feel good about something they or their dog have done. You can bet this positive emotion will serve as motivation to continue on to your next class level!

Difficult Personality Types

We're All Human

While a dog may learn at a slow pace, have aggression issues or be downright obnoxious, he still will not push our buttons the way some people do. Each of us, being human, has sensitivities and areas of low tolerance. In the best of all worlds, we would always be professional and upbeat with our clients; our personal triggers would never get tripped.

The reality is, certain personality types can make it difficult to keep one's composure. Perhaps your usual reaction when someone disagrees with you is to become argumentative. Maybe those know-it-all types irk you no end because your ex-spouse was that way. Perhaps clients who are emotionally needy make you cringe, yet they don't affect the next trainer in the least. We each have our areas of low tolerance, and an Achilles heel or two. The trick is to recognize them and learn how to deal with people who trigger them.

Unless you do board and train only, dog training is really about training people. Doing so effectively can sometimes call for the verbal and psychological equivalent of fancy footwork. As previously mentioned, you do not need a degree in psychology or social work in order to work with people effectively. What you do need is empathy, an understanding of various personality types, and a plan for dealing with them in a productive manner.

Anyone can be difficult. Just look in the mirror. We all say things in ways we don't mean, get cranky when we're ill, and have bad days. Keeping that in mind when a client becomes difficult can help us remain calm and compassionate instead of being reactive.

Much of what follows deals with how to react when clients do or say certain things. And you know, clients do say the darndest things, some of which won't fall into any of the categories described. For example, I had a client once who proudly informed me the reason his dog was so good with children was that he had never let the dog play with dolls. I kid you not. When I asked him to clarify, he explained that because the dog hadn't ever chewed on anything that looked like a child, he would never bite one. If there is a proper response to that one, it escaped me. I remember murmuring something about that being very interesting and moving on. Being a trainer sure does help you develop a poker face.

Although the personality types presented here are clear-cut, people are not. You might have a client who is part Know-It-All Ned and part Argumentative Al, a guy who argues constantly because he is convinced he is right and needs to prove it. A Needy Nita might also be a Rambling Rose.

Just for the record, although I have presented people like Argumentative Al as male and Needy Nita as female, there are assuredly both males and females that fit each of these categories. Each of us displays some of these personality traits from time to time. The problem occurs when a trait gets so out of balance, it dominates a personality.

We cannot change someone's personality, nor is it our job to try. We can, however, control our reactions in hopes of affecting that person's responses to and interactions with us. Just as some people bring out the best or worst in us, we can bring out the best or worst in others. Following are some suggestions that will help in your dealings with clients, whatever their personality type.

Ten Hot Tips for Keeping Your Cool

1. *Be a good listener.* Let the client speak. Don't interrupt and don't disagree. You can always set the record straight later if necessary. Repeating some of what the client has said as part of your response is helpful. It conveys that you have listened and understood.

2. *Be aware of your voice.* Your tone communicates at least as much as your words. We all know the same phrase can be spoken sincerely or sarcastically and mean two very different things. Be aware too of your rate of speech. Speaking slowly has the effect of calming others. Don't respond to shrill, fast-talking clients by raising your pitch and speed to match theirs. (This is one case where you do *not* want to blend.) Maintain an even tone and speak slowly.

3. *Be aware of your body language and your clients'.* Their words might be saying one thing while their body language says another. If you ask whether Gina thinks a certain protocol would be feasible and she's sitting back in a chair, arms and legs crossed, a slight smirk playing at the corner of her mouth as she answers "Sure," it might not convey the affirmative the word implies.

   Your body language, too, communicates volumes. Leaning slightly forward as Gina speaks and nodding your head when appropriate, shows interest. Contrast that with how she would feel if you were to glance around the room as she spoke, arms folded, barely focusing on her. Dogs aren't the only masters of reading body language. Be aware of the subconscious signals you may be sending, and pay attention to those you pick up.

4. *Ignore behavior you don't want and reward behavior you do want.* Sound familiar? This basic principle applies to people as well as dogs. Be careful not to reward unwanted verbal behavior by laughing, smiling or murmuring "mm-hmm". It doesn't matter that you're doing it because you are uncomfortable or trying to be polite; it could be construed as a reward.

   Just as different dogs perceive different things as rewarding, different people find different responses rewarding. For some personality types, arguing with them would be a great reward. Regardless of the type of difficult behavior your clients demonstrate, ignore it and reward them for acting in ways you do want.

5. *Don't become defensive.* Remember, this is not about you. Difficult people are often unaware of how they affect others. Do not respond to a verbal assault, insult or challenge to your authority by becoming defensive. Answering in kind would only escalate the conflict. Instead, do as author Sandra Crowe suggests in her excellent book, *Since Strangling Isn't An Option*...(see *Resources*) and "wear your good attitude like armor." Don't let someone's negativity drag you down. Maintain your level by keeping a positive demeanor.

6. *Redirect unwanted behavior.* Yep, it's another training principle that applies to humans as well as dogs. Instead of arguing with the irritable woman in your class, give her something constructive to do. It's tough to whine and complain as you're counting out homework sheets. Redirecting, when done with grace and subtlety, is extremely effective in keeping things on track and diffusing confrontations.

7. *Act as if.* If you find yourself dealing with a person who is particularly challenging, think of someone you know who would handle the situation well. Then, pretend you are that person. For example, I have a friend who is a good trainer, but has a very passive personality. She finds it extremely difficult to put her foot down with clients. So when she gets into a difficult situation, she imagines she is a mutual trainer friend of ours, a woman who is quite assertive. She pretends to be that trainer—and it works. She is *acting as if.* Doing this repeatedly will help her to become more assertive, and eventually she won't have to pretend.

8. *"Difficult" is a matter of perception.* Judging people rude, obnoxious or otherwise difficult can impede our ability to deal with them effectively. When we label people, our perceptions of any future actions are colored by that initial assessment. Our responses will be as well.

   Try to give people the benefit of the doubt. Someone might be acting rudely; that doesn't mean he or she is a rude person in general. Just as we realize dogs *display* aggressive behaviors rather than simply *being aggressive*, we should strive to see people as displaying certain behaviors on a particular day, rather than simply being that way.

9. *Draw the Line.* Although one can become proficient at dealing with difficult personality types, there comes a time to draw the line. There is a difference between a client who is argumentative and one who is verbally abusive; some simply won't be motivated; others will challenge everything you say; and some are just downright unpleasant. If you feel the person is one you absolutely can not deal with, don't. Simply explain you do not feel it is possible to continue the relationship. Be

47

professional and polite. Say, for example, "I feel it would be best for you and Rusty to work with a trainer whose personality gels better with yours." If the person gets angry, remain calm and simply repeat your statement.

10. *Don't Lose Your Empathy.* We trainers often vent to each other about difficult clients. Let's face it, we all need sympathy and support now and then, and blowing off steam can be a healthy release. Just be sure venting is not all you're doing. Try not to lose your empathy for your clients. Like us, they are doing the best they can.

By being compassionate rather than judgmental, you will ultimately be helping the dogs. Besides, learning to deal with difficult people can not only help us become better trainers, but also to grow as human beings.

Know-It-All Ned and Argumentative Al

Ned must have been a dog expert in a past life. He rejects your suggestions one after another in favor of some inner wisdom that guides him. Why have Roxy stay for five measly seconds when he just knows she can do it for thirty? Why use those pesky food treats when a swift leash jerk gets faster results? Ned might even begin your first appointment by announcing what the dog's problem is, why she's doing it, and whose fault it is. Sometimes you wonder why Ned bothered to call you at all.

Some Neds really are knowledgeable on a variety of topics, while others try to appear so because of their own insecurities. (We all do this to some extent—after all, who wants to appear ignorant?) Ned may attempt to dominate the conversation and can be condescending to those around him, including his family and friends. The thing is, Ned really isn't a bad guy. He is intelligent and is probably even fun to be around when he's not busy pontificating. Just keep in mind that you will never change Ned and it is not your job to try.

Be aware that Ned is a guy with something to prove, so go gently and don't bruise his ego. It can be tempting to put Ned in his place by whipping out a long string of jargon, or making a wry comment that would wipe the smirk off his face. Unfortunately, like the dog that repeatedly jumps and nips, you are more likely to escalate the behavior by feeding into it. Besides, *you* are the professional here, the calm, wise leader. In a social pack structure, the true alpha does not sink to the level of the wanna-be's who are constantly squabbling to prove themselves. If necessary, calmly thank Ned for his opinions and move on.

Great things can happen when you acknowledge Ned's "knowledge"; it doesn't hurt to throw him a bone now and then. Suppose you are working on the recall. Ned proclaims he has done this with many dogs and furthermore, dogs always come when he calls. Alas, you suspect this may not be entirely true. You could point out that the threatening voice he is calling the dog with certainly wouldn't get *you* to come running, but why put him on the defensive? Instead, tell Ned how wonderful it is that he has put in all that time training other dogs. If you can, find something about what he is doing to compliment him on. Perhaps he uses the hand signal well; or he has good timing on the delivery of the treat.

If you can not find anything about Ned to compliment, say something nice about his dog. For example, Roxy is obviously very attentive to him, or she has a beautifully fast response time. Then, with Ned's ego stroked, casually suggest you've got some tips and new techniques you would like to share, to add to his considerable knowledge base. *Then* explain about the need to change his tone of voice, etc.

Another tactic that can be helpful when dealing with Ned is to repeat some of what he has said. That way, he knows he's been heard, and can relax and hopefully process new information. Even if you disagree with what he is saying, repeat some of it back in your response. For example, Ned says, "Dogs love being patted roughly on top of the head." Instead of snapping, "Actually Ned, many dogs don't," you could say, "You're right. There *are* some dogs who love being patted roughly on top of the head. But see the way Roxy licks her lips and turns away? She's telling you she finds it a bit stressful."

Be sure to use phrases that are not antagonistic or commanding.

"Why don't we try…" will get you much further with Ned than "You need to…" With you and Ned on the same team, it will be a lot easier to make progress.

Because Ned probably won't ask many questions (and why should he, since he's already got all the answers), fill in the blanks for him. If there is a subject clients usually ask a common question about, bring it up. For example, when suggesting they use the dog's crate to give a time out, many clients ask whether the dog will then start hating the crate. So when discussing this with Ned, offer, "By the way, a lot of people wonder whether using the crate as a time out will make the dog dislike the crate. So I just want to explain that…" There. You have given Ned important information, and he didn't have to go out on a limb to ask for it. (By the way, the answer is that as long as the dog is already used to and likes his crate, there is no reason timing him out there will cause him to dislike it. After all, when we send a child to his room he doesn't suddenly start to dislike his room.)

In a class situation, since Ned knows so much, he might go so far as to attempt to "help" other students. Just as you would with a dog who is getting into things he shouldn't, redirect. Give Ned something else to do, be it a task with his own dog, or if necessary, a task you invent on the spur of the moment. "Ned, would you help me to move these chairs back against the wall?" is so much more pleasant than "Ned, could you please stop sticking your nose in everyone else's business?"

Since Ned has a low tolerance for being contradicted, you are always better off going with the flow of his ego than struggling against the tide. That can be difficult at times. Just keep in mind you are there not only for Ned's sake, but for the sake of his dog. Part of dealing with Ned is learning when to let things go.

Be sure *you* don't ever become a Know-It-All Ned. Yes, you should be knowledgeable. But if you don't know the answer to a question a client asks, say so. I have a lot more respect for a professional who tells me he does not know the answer but will find out for me, than one who pretends to know it all.

First cousin to Know-It-All Ned is Argumentative Al. In fact, Ned and Al go out for beers together. Of course, Ned always knows the best places to go and Al gets into brawls. Al has been standing on the sidelines as we discuss Ned, shaking his head and biting his tongue. He can barely restrain himself. It's not that Al knows it all like Ned does. It's just that he would love to jump into a heated discussion about Ned's issues; or about anything, for that matter. Sometimes Al argues because he thinks he knows better. Other times it is because Al simply likes to debate. Sometimes Al's "debating" gets so heated that people are temped to call him by another name that starts with "a".

Some guys like Al are married to a female version of themselves. These Alisons also like to argue and boy, the fur sure does fly around their house. But mostly, they don't mean anything by it. They're used to each other. You, however, might be taken aback by their "discussion stylings". (For a more in-depth look at this family dynamic, see *Chapter 15*). More often, Al has married an Agreeable Annie. Annie might not actually agree with what Al is saying, but she has learned that silence is the better part of valor, and that she can do what she wants as long as she lets Al think he has won. There is much to be learned from Annie.

When Al argues, if possible, ignore it; redirect him to something else. Whatever you do, don't take the bait. Following is a conversation I had with a client who was part Know-It-All Ned and part Argumentative Al. I avoided conflict by using humor.

Me: "Let's teach Chester to lie down."
(I begin to lure Chester from a sitting position,
down toward the ground.)

Al: "You know, when I taught Chester to Sit I didn't have
to use treats. Why should I use them to teach him
to lie down?"

Me: "It's great that you taught Chester to sit. Let me show
you how easy using treats will make teaching the down."

Al: "Actually, I can get him to lie down already."

Me: "Oh! I wasn't aware of that. Would you like to show me?"

Al approached Chester, who was now standing. Al bent forward, placed his right arm on Chester's rear and pressed down while chanting, "Sit! Sit! Sit!" Finally, Chester sat. Al then placed his left arm under both of Chester's front legs and swooped them forward, while commanding, "Down!" This caused Chester to plop into a down.

Me (grinning widely):
"Wow! I'll bet if you picked him up and whirled
him around a few times, you could teach him to fly!"

Al's entire family, Al included, burst into peals of laughter. His five-year-old found it particularly amusing. No kidding, I could not get the kid to stop laughing for a full two minutes. Now, mind you, this could have gone either way and I absolutely do not recommend using humor that might criticize or embarrass a client in any way. Just as any tool can be acceptable to one dog and aversive to another, so can humor and mild sarcasm with your human clients. At the time I knew I could get away with it, and it diffused the confrontation. It also made a point. Note too that when I asked Al if he would like to demonstrate what he had said he could do, it was said in a pleasant manner rather than in a confrontational, "Oh yeah? Show me" tone. The end result was we taught Chester to lie down using the treat lure, and both Al and Chester did fabulously.

You will never, ever win by engaging in a verbal sparring match with Al. Besides, what is the best that could come of it? That you win the argument? Al certainly won't be happy about that. You might win the battle but you will have lost the war. And the dog will be the one who ultimately loses in what should never have been a war in the first place. Don't allow yourself to become defensive. Stay focused on solving the problem at hand. Of course, should Al or Ned say something that is truly off-base, by all means set the record straight, in a non-confrontational manner.

Talking with Al or Ned is similar to the art of Tai Chi, where one learns to send negative energy harmlessly on its way, rather than confronting and engaging it. Let Ned and Al have their say. Listen to them. Nod politely. Bite your tongue if you must. Then take a breath and move on to something constructive.

Needy Nita

Nita is basically a nice person. She just happens to have a deep well of issues and insecurities that she is forever trying to fill with emotional contact. If you are not careful, you will be sucked into that well and even Lassie will not be able to pull you out. Nita's emotional neediness should be a problem for her therapist to deal with. But since you are in a relationship of sorts with her, if you are not careful it could become your problem, too.

Nita was a client of mine years ago. She lived with her husband and a lovely, under-exercised Australian Shepherd mix named Wylie. Although Wylie had some minor issues such as pulling on leash, they were nothing that could not have been resolved by increasing his exercise, implementing a leadership program and working with him a bit. Instead of spending time between appointments working with Wylie, however, Nita spent that time calling me. Wylie had jumped on the bed; Wylie had chased the neighbor's cat; Wylie had made a funny sound she couldn't quite identify as a belch, and did I think she should be concerned?

Nita did not really need advice. She wanted to chat. At our appointments, she would seamlessly segue from a discussion of getting Wylie to walk nicely by her side, into a story about a friend she thought would be by her side forever, who had, alas, left. Nita was really good at it, too. By the time she was done she had your ear *and* your sympathy. I have to admit, when she discontinued training due to financial hardship, it was a relief. Nita had been a bit of an energy vampire, and I was drained. I did not deal well with Nitas at the time.

You are not Nita's therapist, nor her confidant. She, however, is not convinced of that. The worst part is, you feel badly for her, so you listen. Every now and then you even find yourself murmuring words of support. Unfortunately, that only encourages Nita. You might feel obligated to do favors for her, or to go further out of your way than you normally would for a client. Don't start down that road—it never ends. (Months after I had stopped working with Nita, I heard that a kindly pet sitter I had referred her to was currently doing twice-weekly visits to walk Wylie for her at no charge. Nita strikes again.) The best defense against getting sucked into Nita's well of neediness is to kindly but firmly keep her on track. When she launches into a personal story during a private appointment, do not comment. When she makes a thinly veiled plea for you to help her in some way above and beyond that of a normal business relationship, ignore it.

If you find Nita calling you night and day between appointments, keep the calls brief. Tell her you were just walking out the door or do not have the time to chat at the moment. Or, suggest Nita keep a list of all the concerns she has during the week so you can address them at the next session. This puts the onus on her to actually do something, and gives her a place to channel all that energy. Each time you say you have to go and she says, "Just one more thing…" calmly suggest she add it to the list.

In a group class setting, Nita might get there early, stay late, or both. While she might not be forward enough to ask questions during class, you will certainly hear from her before or after. The key is to set limits. Some trainers arrive fifteen minutes before class starts and stay fifteen minutes afterward, and will accept questions during those times. Others announce they will be available for consult by phone in-between classes only. This forces students to take the initiative, and the less pressing questions are often weeded out this way. Just be sure if you choose to make yourself available between appointments or classes, that you set a time limit on phone calls. In a group class, announce the rules at the beginning of class so no one feels you are rebuffing him personally when he tries to take too much of your time. Instead, simply remind him of the rules.

During class, Nita may try to monopolize your time. If you have assistants who work with each person individually, you might not have to deal with Nita directly. But whoever does must be sure not to get sucked into the spinning vortex of neediness that surrounds her. Otherwise, the assistant might end up there for fifteen minutes trying to extract herself from Nita's clutches as she pleads, "Just one more thing…" Trainer Donna Duford has an excellent technique for dealing with this type of situation: Instead of approaching Nita closely, call out advice to her as you walk by at a distance. Brilliant! Nita gets the necessary advice, and you get to stay safely out of range. (Of course, your advice would be framed in a positive light so as not to embarass Nita.)

I have been guilty of feeding into Nita's neediness in the past. As someone who is very empathetic and has a hard time saying no to favors, it is sometimes difficult for me to set boundaries. However, after having become way too emotionally involved too many times, I finally learned my lesson. There is nothing wrong with bending over backward to help your friends and loved ones. And it is fine to help your clients too, to a certain degree. Just don't mistake the latter for the former. It is critical to keep your own emotional balance so you can go on to train another day.

*"There are two types of people—those who
come into a room and say, 'Well, here I am!'
and those who come in and say, 'Ah, there you are.'"*

- Unknown

"Everybody wants to get into the act."

- Jimmy Durante

Look-At-Me Leah

Leah is an attention-seeking missile. Although she is an adult, she sometimes acts like the four-year-old who parades around during your in-home appointment pulling out all her toys to show you, or the nine-year-old who turns cartwheels across the carpet while you are teaching the dog to lie down. Leah might as well be wearing a T-shirt that declares, "It's All About ME!"

When Leah's friends call, they barely get a word in edgewise. Anything they say results in the conversation being quickly steered back to Leah. When Nancy mentions she has had a headache all day, Leah responds that she's had a migraine for three. Yes, friends, Leah is a bit of a drama queen. And when she tells her friends about your training class, you can bet it won't be, "Buddy did so well on his down-stay" but rather, "You should have been there at the Musical Chairs game. I smiled at the guy walking the dog next to me to distract him, and when he smiled back I grabbed the last chair!" We all know a Leah.

Like Nita, in a group class setting Leah is likely to ask lots of questions. But while Nita would rather get you alone to talk one-on-one, Leah wants to ask question after question in front of everyone. She doesn't care about the answers so much as the fact that all eyes are on her as she does the asking. Leah might ask questions or make comments that are inappropriate, which can be uncomfortable in a private session and embarrassing for you or your students in a group class. She might laugh too loudly or cause a scene. It is very possible Leah will repeatedly show up late for your group class (all the better to make a Grand Entrance, my dear). And since she is a bit of an exhibitionist, don't be surprised if when she arrives, Leah is dressed flamboyantly.

59

Don't get me wrong. Leah can be likable, funny and even charming. When you spend time with her, there's never a dull moment. But her "look at me" attitude wears thin, and more importantly, does not serve the higher purpose of accomplishing any actual training.

Whether in private training or a group class, do not reward Leah's attention-seeking behavior by acknowledging it. Just as we do with dogs, ignore it and reward appropriate behavior with attention and positive reinforcement. (Keep in mind that like an "extinction burst" from an attention-seeking dog that is being ignored, Leah's behavior might escalate before it finally stops.) Remember that even negative attention, such as asking Leah to be quiet or even glancing at her, is attention.

While others are quietly practicing down-stays, Leah loudly complains that her hot-pink leash keeps getting tangled. If she truly needs help, quietly give it. If not, ignore it. When students are asked to share how the training went during the week, Leah constantly comments on the stories of others. Ignore it. Any response would be encouraging to her.

We do not, however, want Leah to feel constantly shot down and frustrated. So she wants the spotlight? Let's give it to her! If there is something Leah and her dog do particularly well, ask them to demonstrate for the class. Or, call everyone's attention to them by saying, "Did you see the way Leah kept Buddy's leash nice and slack as they walked? That's what we're aiming for!" Leah gets the attention she so craves, and the class stays on track.

Sometimes giving your difficult personality types just a little bit of what they crave, on your terms, helps to keep peaceable relations.

Rambling Rose

Sister to Nita and Leah is Rambling Rose. Once Rose gets to talking, you'd best grab a cup of tea and settle in. Leah, of course, cuts Rose off brusquely because it's not all about her. Nita happily lets Rose talk as long as she likes, basking in the glow of Rose's companionship.

Of course, in a private training session or group class, the last thing you want to let Rose do is ramble. Be careful not to feed into it by nodding your head or offering polite "uh-huh"s. That will only encourage her. When Rose launches into a story about "the cutest thing Frankie did the other day, you should have seen it, we were coming out of the store, blah, blah, blah...." cut her off at the pass. It's the only thing to do. Then, quickly redirect! There is no need to be rude about it. Simply wait for Rose to stop for a breath, then jump in quickly with something along the lines of, "That's an interesting story, Rose, but let's get back to Frankie's 'go to bed' exercise. He's just starting to get it and I don't want to lose our momentum."

If Rose interrupts repeatedly during a private session, going off on tangents and launching into anecdotes, you must take control. Be kind and gentle. "Rose," you might suggest, "I think it would be best, since we have limited time together, to keep on track. I want you and Frankie to get the most out of our training sessions as possible." If necessary, you could also remind her she is paying you by the hour.

If you are teaching a group class and Rose launches into yet another long personal story, cut her off politely and redirect the group as a whole to the next activity. Even if you have done so previously, at the beginning of the next class remind everyone questions are welcome—but only if they are on topic and only in the context of a general question.

If Rose starts rambling in class while students are practicing with their dogs, give her something to do. Suppose your students are practicing leashwork. "Rose," you could interject, "You're doing great. Now for this exercise, I'd like you to take exactly ten steps in-between asking Scruffy to sit. Be sure to count them!" Can *you* chat and count at the same time? I can't. It is important not to let Rose monopolize class time. If she does, you will end up frustrated and your students will wonder why the instructor doesn't have better control of the class. If necessary, speak with Rose privately after class. Explain things to her gently but firmly.

Be aware that Rose is probably overly verbal where her dog is concerned as well. She might instruct Frankie to sit by asking, "Frankie, sit; come on, sit; come on, sit down now…" It is important that you make Rose understand verbosity is not productive in training. I ask talkative clients whether they remember Charlie Brown's teacher in the Peanuts cartoon series. Most adults recall the way the kids heard, "wah-wah-wah" regardless of what the teacher was actually saying. I then tell the owner, "That's what your dog is hearing, lots of wah-wah-wah." That usually elicits a chuckle—and a light bulb going on over the owner's head. You could also suggest Rose give the cue, followed immediately by a deep breath. You might be surprised at how quickly this technique leads to one-word cues. After all, even Rose can't take a breath and talk at the same time.

Take care that you don't become a Rambling Rose yourself. It can be tempting to regale your clients with fascinating anecdotes from your training experiences or personal life. While clients might find these digressions interesting and even encourage them, storytelling is not conducive to staying on track and giving clients the most for their money. But if you have a short story that is pertinent, by all means, tell it. It might help someone to retain information or understand the significance of an exercise.

When stressing the importance of teaching a solid recall, I often tell clients how doing so saved my German Shepherd's life: Ten years ago, when Soko was still a pup, we took her to the beach. This particular Southern California beach runs along the Pacific Coast Highway, a very busy stretch of road with cars flying by at 70-90 mph. Drivers park on the shoulder, with the beach on one side and the highway on the other. I drove a small Honda Civic wagon back then and Soko rode in the folded-seat rear area. (And yes, she should have been crated or strapped in.) I parked. My husband opened the beach-side door and bent to tie his shoelace. In a flash, Soko leaped into the front seat, ran out the door and headed into traffic. I jumped out and began to rush after her. Then I caught myself. I stood still and, in my best "we're training now" voice, called, "Soko!" When she turned toward me, I gave the hand signal and said, "Come!" Thanks to persistent training (and a bit of divine intervention I will always be grateful for), Soko turned on a dime and came running back to me, unharmed. Pretty dramatic stuff. I can tell this story in under two minutes. Hopefully it will make clients understand the importance of the recall enough to motivate them to really work on it. And who knows, one day it might even save their dogs' life.

Contrast the previous story with a lengthy one that begins, "Once when I was training recalls in the park with a friend, we had the dogs on long lines and another dog came out of nowhere and everyone got tangled and..." Who cares? While it might be entertaining, how does that serve the client? If you are going to share a story, be sure it is pertinent. Even if it doesn't make a dramatic point, perhaps it lets the person know everyone is fallible, even you. If John is getting frustrated with trying to get Rex to walk on leash nicely, sharing a story about how your dogs once got you so tangled in their leashes you almost fell down might put him at ease. Use your own judgement, but whatever story you choose to share, don't become a Rambling Rose!

Regardless of whether your client is Needy Nita, Look-At-Me Leah or Rambling Rose, the best thing you can do is remain focused. Just as with a high-energy dog who constantly jumps and mouths, your becoming flustered will only escalate the situation. Be calm and consistent. Rose and the others will eventually modify their behavior, at least around you. And that's all you can ask.

Unmotivated Mo and Ditzy Diane

Mo and Diane have a ten-month-old Labrador Retriever named Bob. Mo thought it would be cute to name the dog Bob. He also thought having a dog would be a lot less work. Mo works hard enough at his job! Besides, if he's paying a dog trainer, the dog should be getting trained without him, right? The last three trainers didn't seem to understand that.

Diane understands Bob won't train himself between appointments. It's just that she's got so many things going on. She can't find the time to practice with him, and she can never seem to remember what that nice trainer said to do when Bob steals food from the table or gets overly mouthy. Mo remembers but doesn't feel like going to the bother of giving Bob a time out. When you return for a second appointment and ask whether the changes you had suggested are helping, Bob and Diane smile and chime, "Sure!" But when you ask specifically whether they have switched Bob from being free-fed to eating twice daily, Diane sheepishly replies in the negative. Started taking him for walks? "We will, we just haven't yet" offers Mo. Practiced his stays? "Whoops, forgot about that one" answers Diane. What's a trainer to do?

Unmotivated clients are the bane of trainers everywhere. They conjure visions of a dog pulling its owner down the street and jumping on a passerby, who exclaims, "You ought to get that dog trained!" to which the owner responds, "We did! We went to (insert your name here)." None of us want that kind of advertising. Many unmotivated owners go from trainer to trainer, expecting the trainers to do the work for them, complaining when they don't. I'll admit that when I used to get calls saying, "I've been to three other trainers and none of them could fix Buddy's problem," I would mentally don my red cape and proclaim, *Supertrainer to the rescue! Those other trainers were mere mortals who used ineffective methods! I can dodge speeding Labradors! I can fix unwanted leaping in a single bound!* Let me tell you about those mere mortals. They may or may not have been good trainers, but you can bet the owners did not follow through with anything they suggested. Be careful that you do not end up added to the failed trainer litany that will be recited to the next trainer.

Many trainers refuse to work with unmotivated clients, period. They will tell owners in no uncertain terms that unless they get in line and start working with the dog, they should find another trainer. I can understand that. Before I get to that point, though, unless I think the situation is completely hopeless, I will try to find a way to make things work. This does not mean continually accepting excuses or a total lack of effort. It means understanding this is the real world and people have busy lives. And it doesn't hurt to remember that we are all human and sometimes we need a little help to get where we need to go.

Three Keys to Success

You will get much further with the Mos and Dianes of the world if you:

1. Break things into small, achievable pieces.
2. Convince them there is something in it for them.
3. Show immediate results, no matter how small.

Breaking things down into small pieces was discussed in *Chapter Three*, so let's skip directly to point two. Many of us naturally use the skill of influencing people by pointing out what's in it for them if they go along with our suggestions. A trainer friend of mine (no really, it only *seems* like all my friends are trainers) had a problem with mold in her house. Now, "a fungus among us" is not a thing to be taken lightly. However, all attempts at getting her husband to help deal with the problem were met with placating remarks and procrastination. When she finally suggested the mold might be contributing to his asthma and if they got rid of it he would feel much better, the problem was addressed in record time.

When Mo gets home from work, he does not want to be bothered to take Bob for a walk. Truth be told, Mo is irritated from the time Bob jumps all over his good suit as he walks in, to the time Bob finally settles down. Mo just wants to come home and relax! You could suggest since Diane gets home earlier than Mo, she take Bob for a long walk. That way, he is tired out by the time Mo gets home. Besides, Diane has mentioned needing some exercise herself, so there is something in it for her. Paint a picture for Mo and Diane of spending a nice, peaceful evening at home, Diane and Bob pleasantly worn out after their walk, Mo relaxing in his easy chair.

No matter what you are trying to achieve with the dog, paint a detailed picture for the owners of the end result. Why put the time and energy into teaching a stay? Because, you explain, then Bob could sit-stay when Mo walks in the door, instead of jumping on him. Bob could also sit-stay while having his leash put on for a walk. And those down-stays will allow Mo and Diane to eat their dinner in peace. *That sure would be nice*, thinks Mo. *This might be worth a little time and effort after all.*

Now we get to number three, immediate results. Although you are working to improve Bob's greeting behavior, Mo needs to see some improvement now, not weeks down the road. So you suggest that until Bob reliably sits to greet people, he be tethered to the hall bannister whenever the doorbell rings. They can then play "Remote Control Butt": With Bob tethered, guests enter. As long as Bob is sitting, guests may approach and greet him. If Bob's rear comes off the ground, guests are to ignore him until he resumes sitting. You demonstrate. When Mo sees how well this works, he becomes less stressed and more optimistic about training. He can envision Bob doing this off tether if they keep working at it. Diane is thrilled. Bob is hard for her to handle physically, particularly at the door. She hadn't thought of tethering him. This will make having the girls over much easier, too.

When dealing with unmotivated clients, regardless of how much lecturing you do at the first session, be sure to show tangible proof that the dog can learn something. Sit and Down are fast and simple to teach, and the quick results will encourage enthusiasm and compliance. "Leave it" is another one I love to teach right away, because owners are often amazed their dog gets it so quickly. I love to see owners beam with pride as they realize how smart their dogs are. I had one client who truly thought her dog was hopeless. She was so happy and relieved to find he could actually learn something, she cried. It was great.

Targeting—in this case teaching the dog to touch the back of your hand with his nose—is another easily achievable behavior. When teaching targeting, be sure to explain the applications of it, i.e. by doing it when walking, it can work into a nice heel. I am also sure to mention targeting is great for teaching tricks and share that I taught my fur-kid, Mojo, to turn out the lights using this method. That never fails to impress owners and definitely motivates them to want to train their dog. Of course, you do not want to teach things the dog truly doesn't need to learn or in which the client has no interest. But chances are, if he has not learned these basic skills (with the debatable exception of targeting), he needs to.

The need for achieving early success does not apply only to the dogs. Showing clients early on that *they* can accomplish something is equally important. The more quickly they become proficient, even at the little things, the more confident they will be and the more likely to continue the program.

A Tracking a Day Keeps the Slacking At Bay

Record keeping helps clients see progress and stay motivated. It need not be time-consuming or complicated. Let's say Buddy has been nipping the kids. Instruct your owners that each time he nips, Buddy should be given a time out. They are to keep track of how many time outs Buddy gets each evening. Be sure they are comparing apples to apples. If Buddy and the kids are always indoors on weekdays from 6:30 to 9:30 p.m., keeping track of how many time outs Buddy gets during those hours each night is a fair comparison. If the amount of time Buddy spends in the kids' presence varies daily, the comparison is not valid.

The simplest way to keep track is to make two columns. Note the day of the week in the first, and how many time outs Buddy received in the second. It might look like this:

Day	Time Outs
Sunday	16
Monday	13
Tuesday	9
Wednesday	12
Thursday	8
Friday	9
Saturday	6

If your clients are more industrious and would like to plot Buddy's progress on a graph, it would look like this:

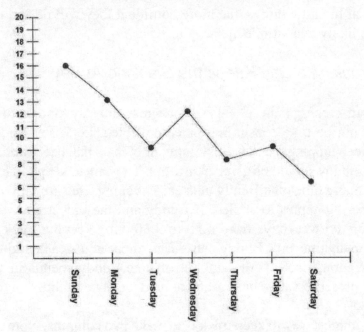

Either way, your clients will see definite progress. Be sure to let them know from the start that progress will not occur in a straight line. In other words, it is normal to have some backsliding. In Buddy's case, the incidence of nipping decreased between Sunday and Tuesday, with a brief resurgence on Wednesday. It then decreased further through Saturday. Contrast the way Buddy's owners would feel after seven days without keeping records (*Gee, you'd think after a week he would have stopped nipping the kids!*) versus seeing the number of time outs go from sixteen to six.

Some clients, especially those with kids, might find another type of progress chart helpful. Trainer Susan Ferry offers, "What I have found to be very successful is to have people put gold or black stars on their calendar. A black star denotes a 'bad behavior' day; a gold one, a good day. When the client stands back and looks at it as a whole, those gold stars stand out prominently and are a great reminder of what they have achieved, as opposed to what has yet to be achieved."

Your clients can chart progress on almost any training or behavior issue. A simple chart for housebreaking could show the number of "accidents" the dog had each day. Jumping up could be charted the same way as nipping. An owner could track how many times Max pulled on leash between Point A and Point B on daily walks. However, more complicated issues, such as dog-dog aggression, would be difficult to chart accurately because there are too many variables. For example, if Max lunges at other dogs on walks, it would be very difficult to control the number of dogs he passes, the distance they are at and other factors. Unless all variables are fixed, I would suggest keeping records for simple issues only.

It's About Time

Let's get back to Mo and Diane. Diane just doesn't get this whole "leadership" thing you want her to do, even though you have explained it and given her a handout outlining the program. She has had so much going on, she hasn't had the time to read it. You could comment that doing so would have taken only five minutes, but why put Diane on the defensive? Instead, help her to build small, simple leadership exercises into her day. Work them into her schedule and *ask whether she thinks they are feasible.*

Remember, it is what Diane is willing and able to do that counts, not what you think she ought to be able to do. Since Diane feeds Bob in the mornings, could she ask him to sit before putting his food bowl down? She replies that would not be a problem. What

71

about walking Bob when she gets home? Diane says most days that would be fine, but Tuesdays are "girls' night out," so she won't be there. You suggest they switch Bob's doggie daycare day from Thursdays to Tuesdays; that way Diane can drop Bob off at home, go out with the girls, and Bob will be tired and mellow when Mo gets home. "Yes!" Diane answers, "That would be great." Help your clients to find realistic, concrete solutions.

For some owners, filling out a calendar can help. Sit down with them and block out any time taken up by sleep, work and regular activities. Then look at the remaining time and with their input, find small increments where they can train, exercise and spend time with their dog. It is possible that when you do this, they will see how little time they are spending at these things. They might then be willing to adjust their schedule or habits, or get a second dog to keep the first company. As a last resort, if the dog is truly suffering from neglect, the calendar (along with your input) might help them to realize that and to make the choice to rehome the dog, which would be the kindest thing to do.

"I Shouldn't Have To!"

With some people it is not that they don't have the time. They just do not feel they should have to put in any effort, since they are paying you. I head this off at the pass by making it clear in the initial phone conversation that I am not going to be taking the dog and training it, but training *them* to train their dog. I stress that the only way the program will be successful is if they put the time and effort into doing short daily training sessions between appointments. If they tell me flat out that will not be possible, I suggest they find another trainer. I add that even if they send the dog for board and train, they still will have to keep up the training once the dog gets home, or they will have wasted their money.

Pick of the Litter - Motivated Clients

Another thing I learned the hard way is how to spot unmotivated clients when scheduling appointments. I used to bend over backward for clients. Let's face it, I needed the work. If someone said she could only see me at 7:30 a.m. before her work day started, even though I did not normally take my first appointment until 9:00, I would make an exception. I would see clients in the mid-to-late evenings, which is far from being my best time of day mentally and energetically. I even took appointments on Sundays, which is the day I spend with my family.

You might be thinking, what's the big deal with being flexible in your hours now and then? The big deal is, if people are not willing to make the effort to fit training into their schedule, whether that means waking up a bit earlier on a Saturday morning or changing a nail appointment, they are not going to be motivated to follow through with your recommendations.

Trainer John Rogerson only sees clients at his office and only at the times he suggests. This immediately ensures a certain level of compliance. Most of us do not have that luxury, but we can still stand firm enough that we select for the more motivated clients from the start. (*Note*: The exception to this rule is aggression cases. For those, I will make every effort, within reason, to work the client into my schedule quickly. Most people call right after the dog has bitten someone, when they are highly motivated to address the issue. As time passes they will sink back into complacency and might cancel the appointment.)

If I arrive at the clients' home week after week only to be met with a total lack of progress and an apathetic, "We just didn't have time to train this week," I will make it clear that unless they make an effort, I will not continue to work with them. There is no point in wasting anyone's time, or their money. Some begin to work with the dog and find it was not as hard as they thought it would be. Others still don't do a thing, and I will drop them as clients. Trying to make progress with a wall of apathy blocking your path is a losing proposition. You may feel that financially, you do not have the luxury of firing unmotivated clients. But weigh the loss of one client against the damage that client could do to your reputation by saying you were an ineffective trainer, or by telling people *you* trained this obviously untrained dog. Better to lose one client now than ten down the road.

There's at Least One in Every Crowd

In a class situation, you will encounter students who have obviously not done their homework. Some will admit they have not had the time or just didn't think about it. One woman actually told me the dog ate her homework! The funny part was, it was true. Whatever the reason, instead of embarrassing or berating your students, highlight and reward those who have obviously worked with their dogs. Make a big deal of it. "I can see you and Cooper have been practicing," you might tell Wendy as Cooper performs a flawless down-stay for all to see. Everyone wants recognition, and you might be surprised at how rewarding those who have made an effort quickly raises the level of cooperation.

Another helpful tactic is to play games based on the previous week's lesson. No one wants to look foolish or lose a game, particularly when there are prizes involved! Weekly games boost motivation for at-home practice. Terry Ryan's booklets *Games People Play..., Life Beyond Block Heeling* and her new comprehensive pet dog instructor's manual (see *Resources*) have excellent ideas for class games.

While we would love for all our students to work with their dogs at home, despite our best efforts, many never will. But even those students need reinforcement to stay motivated. Try to find something positive to comment on, even if it is simply the fact that they showed up to class. After all, they are making the effort to be there.

Here is an example of how one trainer solved a motivation problem in class: Frances Dauster used to mail an evaluation sheet to each student after the last class had ended. Despite the inclusion of a self-addressed envelope, the return rate was only about ten percent. She then tried distributing the forms at the beginning of the last class, to be returned when class ended; she didn't get a single one back. Then Frances had an idea: when students were done filling out the evaluation sheet at the last class, they turned them in and received a chocolate chip cookie in exchange. Ah, the sweet smell of success!

It can be incredibly frustrating to work with unmotivated owners or those who just don't "get it". But the next time you come across a Mo or Diane, give them a break. Maybe no one else has. By being patient and working with them creatively instead of just venting about them later on, everyone, including the dog, will benefit.

"People who never get carried away should be."

- Malcolm Forbes

Bland Betty

It is the last night of your group class. Students and dogs are happily playing games and showing off what they have learned. Everyone is smiling or laughing—everyone, that is, except Bland Betty. Betty has worn the same vacant expression since the very first class. She has not smiled, asked a question, or made a comment; you have no idea what is going on in her mind. Sometimes you wonder whether Betty enjoys training at all.

We all come across Betty types in our group classes and private training. I find the stone-faced contingent particularly challenging. It is difficult not to worry about how you or what you are presenting are being perceived when someone gives no response whatsoever. What I have learned is not to take Bettys at "face value."

I remember one particular Betty in a group class. I had gotten the feeling she wasn't enjoying the training much, and that perhaps she was very dedicated to her dog and therefore willing to put up with class, week after drudging week. After the graduation ceremony, Betty surprised me by coming up to tell me how much she had enjoyed the class. You could have blown me over with a dog hair. The moral is, don't ever assume what someone is thinking.

There are many people who, regardless of what emotion they are feeling, wear a neutral expression. Heck, with the advent of Botox, half the women in Los Angeles look that way! Betty is not a difficult type because of her personality, but because of her seeming lack of one. Ask any performer how important audience feedback is. It is very difficult to give any type of seminar or performance where the audience watches passively. It is human nature to wonder whether one is bombing. We want to see animation, involvement... or at least signs of life!

Don't let Bland Betty throw you for a loop. Put your own need for positive reinforcement on the back burner, and consider that Betty might simply be shy, or naturally quiet and non-demonstrative. Who knows, she might even be on medication that flattens the personality. Whatever you do, try not to get frustrated or angry with her. If you do, especially if Betty is shy, she may retreat further into her shell. Speak softly and do not overwhelm her with too-intense body language. Use blending to match your vocal pattern and body language to hers. Once she feels more at ease, Betty is more likely to open up and respond.

Draw Betty out by asking questions that have to be answered with more than a simple yes or no. For example, in a private session, instead of asking whether she has practiced the down-stay with Cody, ask how far she has gotten with the exercise. Be sure there is no hint of judgement or disapproval in your tone of voice. Watch to see whether your questions are making Betty more comfortable or causing her to shut down, then proceed accordingly. Use humor where appropriate. If you can get Betty to lighten up and laugh a little, you will both feel better. And don't worry about whether she is enjoying the training; if she's not, she'll stop.

As long as she continues to work with you, assume Betty is getting something out of it. Be patient. Who knows, Bland Betty might turn out to be one of those laughing, happy students after all.

Angry Agnes

While Al enjoys a healthy debate and Ned could spend all day pontificating, Agnes can be volatile. She might stew on a low simmer, smirking or shaking her head as you speak, then eventually explode. Or, she might erupt frequently in short, violent outbursts. Either way, Agnes is an angry person. She is probably insecure and is most definitely unhappy. You will never know what is at the root of Agnes' anger and it is not your job to find out. Unfortunately, you might have to deal with her behavior in your group class or private session.

If Agnes attends your group class, her angry outbursts are likely to occur in front of everyone. I had an Agnes in one of my group classes, a deeply unhappy woman who chose to angrily vent about just about everything during class. She would rant about the ineffectiveness of the training methods; about how she still could not get her dog to listen to her after all these classes; and on and on. Angry people have a tendency to blame things on anyone and anything—except, that is, themselves. Regardless of what Agnes said, I tried my best to remain calm and helpful. If she really got out of control, I would smile, look directly at her and say assertively, "I'll be happy to discuss that with you after class." And I would.

Angry people want to be heard, not to be told to calm down or to be quiet. If you admonish Agnes to be quiet or worse, respond in kind, her anger is only going to escalate. Ignoring her outbursts might work temporarily, but remember that ignored behavior can get more intense and erupt into an extinction burst (that off-the-scale tantrum behavior) before it stops completely. You really don't want to chance an extinction burst from Agnes.

79

When faced with Agnes one-on-one, remind yourself to keep breathing evenly. Remain calm and quiet, and let the initial flareup burn itself out. Author Sandra Crowe equates that initial flareup to a lit match and advises, "Your best defense is to let the match burn itself out. Don't argue. Don't agree. Just hang with it. Without fuel, it will extinguish itself." Sound familiar?

Once the initial flareup has passed, let Agnes know she has been heard. You could repeat part of what she has said back to her. Be on her side. After all, it's harder to fight with someone who is not against you. If Agnes exclaims, "This exercise is impossible. How can you expect anyone to do this?" you might reply kindly but assertively, "I understand how frustrating this can be at the beginning. When I started doing this exercise I felt the same way. Let's just try this one part of it first." You have disarmed Agnes by letting her know she has been heard and that you understand and have been there yourself. You then redirected her to doing something productive. Imagine, on the other hand, the effect it might have had if you had responded, "Actually, Agnes, the exercise is not what's impossible. No one else seems to be having a problem with it." You would have put Agnes on the defensive and things would have escalated. Remember that your angry student feels frustrated and probably embarrassed as well. Be kind.

It can be difficult at times to control your own anger when faced with Agnes' onslaught. No matter how angry you feel, breathe deeply and concentrate on diffusing the situation. Speak slowly and evenly. Make every attempt not to loose your cool, no matter what Agnes says. It doesn't matter who is right at that moment. What is important is diffusing the anger so the training can be productive.

Once Agnes is a bit calmer, bring logic into the picture. Stick to facts and steer clear of emotions. For example, Agnes says, "Buster won't stop nipping me. I hate that! I just know he does it for spite!" Now is not the time to explain that dogs don't do things for spite, nor to tell Agnes not to get so upset. Stick to the issue at hand. You could ask calmly, "What have you tried so far to stop the nipping?" If Agnes blurts, "I held his mouth shut. That didn't work either. I'm really at the end of my rope. He should be over this by now!" steer the conversation away from the emotional and back to concrete solutions.

Listening to Agnes' anger burn itself out and then reasoning with her should not be confused with letting Agnes walk all over you. After all, you are the professional and must maintain control. Be focused and assertive. Use your body language to show you are listening but not backing off. Plant your feet firmly and lean slightly forward. Keep your verbal tone firm. If you have an Agnes in class who is truly disruptive, ask privately that she refrain from having these outbursts. If she will not or can not stop, you are certainly within your rights to expel her. In one-on-one training, you can decline to set up further appointments.

Thankfully, I have only had one Agnes over the years who was so volatile that I felt the integrity of the class was at risk. At what was to be the last of many unpleasant post-class private discussions, Agnes informed me she was sick and tired of this "gentle crap," that her husband hit the dog and it listened to him, that she'd gotten nothing out of the class, and so on. She then attacked my training skills and me personally.

After ten minutes of my remaining calm, letting her blow her top and then attempting to have a rational exchange, I finally told Agnes I was going to refund her money for the last two classes and she was not to return. (Technically, I did not have to give a refund but it was worth it to break with her cleanly and permanently.) She seemed surprised. I was actually quite proud of the fact that I was able to remain calm throughout the exchange and handle it in a professional manner, particularly because that little voice in my head was screaming things that were decidedly unprofessional. No matter how angry you are, take the high road.

Dealing with Agnes types on a regular basis can lead to some residual anger of your own. Be sure to find productive ways to release it. Vent to a friend; go home and beat up a pillow; exercise. Do whatever works for you—just don't hold on to it. We all know unresolved anger can contribute to stress and eventually, illness.

Fortunately, most Agnes types are not as common nor as volatile as the one mentioned. We can handle them fairly easily, and by doing so, keep them and their dogs in training. And as with most difficult personality types, learning to deal with Angry Agnes in training situations can yield the priceless benefit of helping us learn to deal with her in all aspects of our lives.

All in the Family

If you have been in the business for any length of time, you have no doubt found yourself in situations where you feel more like a family therapist than a dog trainer. Disagreements arise. Accusations fly. Tempers flare. It can be awkward, to say the least.

In some families, the discord is more subtle. One member might be continually condescending toward or critical of another, or be domineering over all. Couples squabble. You might find yourself caught in the middle as each person demands you tell the other who is right. While it is certainly not your job to get involved in or to solve deep-seated family conflicts, it is helpful to have an idea of how to proceed when the fur starts to fly.

The Family Feud

The Sullivan family—John, Jenny, their three daughters and son— are sprawled across the living room. When you ask how many times a day Rex gets walked, fourteen-year-old Carla offers, "Once". Karen, twelve, jumps in and says, "No he doesn't," to which Jan, nine, replies, "Sometimes Daddy walks him at night." John sighs and says, "He gets about two walks a week. Carla is supposed to walk him in the mornings but she doesn't most of the time." Carla shoots John a withering look as she retorts, "That's because you're in the bathroom so long I don't have time to take a shower and then walk Rex." John tells Carla to be quiet and listen to the trainer. Jenny jumps in to admonish John, "I told you, you take too long in the bathroom in the mornings. I'm even late for work sometimes because of you. How can you expect

Carla to have time to walk Rex?" Uh-oh. This is not leaning toward a friendly family discussion.

Unfortunately, this pattern is far from uncommon. I have taken histories from couples who gave opposite answers to every question. I was sorely tempted to ask, "Do you two actually live in the same house?" It is difficult to get solid information when everyone has a different perspective. Simple disagreements can turn into family squabbles if you are not careful. Your job is to stay neutral and supportive and keep things on track. Above all, do not lay blame.

Breaking problems down can help. In the Sullivan family's case, you might proceed by saying, "Carla, it's great that you're making an effort to take Rex for walks. It sounds as though things are really busy around here in the mornings. What would make this easier for you?" You have let Carla know you understand her situation and can sympathize, and have removed any blame from the equation. You have encouraged cooperation and honest responses. And, you have made Carla feel she has some say in the matter. "Well," Carla offers, "I guess I could walk Rex while Dad's still in the bathroom, then take my shower when I get back." Great! You commend Carla on an excellent idea, confirming with the other family members that the plan sounds workable. Now you ask John whether he could walk Rex a few more times during the week, after he gets home from work. And could John Jr. throw the ball for Rex before school on the mornings Carla can't walk him? Stick with it until you find a solution that works for everyone.

Family schedules are often crammed with activities. Many of the kids I see have busier social lives than their parents! But even in the busiest of families, time can be found. Sit down with a calendar if necessary and write out who will do what, when. Get agreement from all family members. Ensuring that each person has a say in setting the schedule will make it more likely that everyone will comply. Suggest they post the schedule somewhere accessible, i.e. on the fridge, to keep everyone on track.

Trainer in the Middle

Couples will try to pull you into the middle of their disagreements. "Please tell Stu if he keeps encouraging Bonzai to jump on him, we're never going to get him to stop jumping on everyone else" implores Lorna. "What's wrong with him jumping on me?" Stu retorts. "I can get him to stop if I want to. It's the way she tells him to get down that's the problem. She just needs to use a firmer voice, right?" Even if one person is absolutely right and the other wrong, do not take sides. Saying something like, "Actually Stu, Lorna's been right about the last five things so maybe you ought to start listening to her" is not going to help, and will significantly lessen the likelihood of your returning for a second visit.

Do not fault either party. "Stu," you might suggest, "I understand it's fun to have Bonzai jump on you. I've got a big, goofy dog at home I love to do that with. The thing is, I don't want him jumping on other people, or even on me for that matter, when he's not invited. So what if we teach Bonzai first not to jump on anyone including you, then we teach him a signal that means it's okay to jump on you when asked." Stu's face lights up. He won't have to give up Bonzai's jumping altogether. Lorna is relieved.

Now you address the accusation Stu made about Lorna's lack of voice control by touching on the subject in a general way. You tell them both, "Since Bonzai jumps because he wants attention, an easy way to get him to stop jumping would be to ignore him. You don't need to say a word." You then go on to describe the

85

protocol. Nowhere did you say who was right or wrong in so many words. No one is offended, no one loses face, and you have found a solution that satisfies everyone.

We're In This Together, Baby

Whenever possible, get couples playing on the same team. Teach them that to be good leaders for the dog, it is best to present a unified front. That means backing each other up. For example, if Lorna tells Bonzai to get off the couch and he doesn't, instead of Stu making a derisive comment about Lorna's lack of authority, he should help to move Bonzai off the couch. This teaming-up tactic is especially helpful with dogs who challenge one owner's authority.

Another effective way to get couples on the same team is to encourage them to coach each other. As one performs a training exercise, the other gives feedback. Explain the rules clearly at the start. No one is allowed to say the other is "wrong". Constructive criticism and support are welcome, but must be specific. Be sure to give examples of ways to phrase things. For example, instead of saying, "You're doing that all wrong," Stu could say, "Try moving the lure straight down instead of toward you." You will probably have to remind couples of these rules as they go along.

If you can get couples interacting this way, not only will you have made them more effective trainers, but you will have given them a model for having productive discussions in other parts of their relationship. This coaching-and-feedback exercise works for all family members, by the way, not just couples. Always be aware of the personalities involved, and have them do this exercise only if you feel they can handle it.

You Treat Me Like a Dog!

You can learn a great deal about how a family interacts with its dog by observing how its members interact with each other. I recently worked with a woman whose five-year-old daughter kept "acting up" during our private session. The woman asked the child nicely a few times to knock it off. The child kept it up. The woman finally said sternly, "If you don't stop, you're going into time out." The child kept right on going. The woman said, "Okay, that's it, go to time out." The child started whining and crying that she didn't want to. The woman snapped, "Then go sit down and be quiet." What's wrong with this picture? Although I knew her telling the child to go to time out and then backing down was wrong, I did not say a word. Later on, when discussing giving her dog a time out for nipping, I was sure to emphasize that once she gives the verbal cue, "Time out" she must follow through, or the dog will learn that her words mean nothing. She did not comment, but I saw a slight nod and a look in her eye that I suspect meant she had put two and two together.

Commenting on someone's parenting skills or family relationship, regardless of how it relates to dog training, is a touchy proposition at best. Don't do it. Make a mental note of any pertinent family dynamic you observe and proceed accordingly. Keeping quiet can be difficult at times, especially as some family situations you encounter might strike a nerve.

You might even see dynamics you have experienced in your own family played out before your eyes. This happened to me in a group class I taught years ago. There was a father and his ten-year-old daughter. Any time the girl worked with the dog, the father became hypercritical of her performance. His words could not be considered constructive criticism by a long shot. Normally,

87

I would have had the father doing the exercises first and then coaching his daughter, but try as I might, the father refused to participate, saying, "It's her dog. She needs to work with it." For seven weeks, I watched this guy berate his daughter, and watched her pained reaction. As you might imagine, I felt terrible for her. I knew I could not change the father. So I went out of my way to support the daughter whenever possible, pointing out what she was doing right and helping to shape things in the direction of her doing them even better. I made sure the father heard the positive comments.

I sincerely hope that no matter how much the father might criticize her at home, that little girl will always remember the trainer telling her how well she did. And I hope that on some level the father realized his daughter did better when she was supported instead of criticized. Again, it is not our place to fix family problems, but if we can be a positive force for family dynamics while training the dog, all the better.

It is ironic that although our job is to teach clients how to effectively work with their dogs, by doing so we are also helping them to learn to communicate better with each other. Maybe we are family therapists after all.

Working with Kids

Communicating with kids may come naturally to you. Perhaps you have kids yourself, or are around them a lot. Or maybe you are more like me and many other dog trainers. All my kids have four feet! (I even had T-shirts printed that say so.) I do not have relatives or friends with kids who visit, and although I like kids well enough, I am not what you would call a "kid person". But whether you love kids or can barely tolerate them (like my friend who suggested I call this chapter "Spawn of Satan and How to Train Them"), becoming adept at communicating with and motivating kids will make you a more effective trainer. After all, most of us are training family pets, and most families have children.

If the children you are working with are of school age, you have a distinct advantage—they already have a student-teacher model in their lives. They might well follow suggestions from you, the teacher, more than they would from their parents. The whole school model strikes me funny; I always find it a little strange yet endearing when a child raises a hand to ask a question during a training session. But there are advantages to playing the teacher role, including being in a good position to give kids homework to do with the dog.

Think back to when you were in school. Can you remember your favorite teacher? My memory is so bad I couldn't tell you what I had for breakfast this morning, but I can still remember Mr. Delman, my seventh grade music teacher. He was eccentric and brilliant and had a huge influence on me. Most of us had at least one teacher we liked and who influenced us. Wouldn't it be great if we could be that teacher for our clients' kids? Sure, we are

89

there to train the dog, but it sure helps in gaining trust and cooperation to be someone kids like.

Kids are Not Invisible

Some trainers who are not around kids much tend to ignore them at training sessions. Sure, a two-year-old child is not likely to contribute much. But for those who are old enough, don't treat them as though they aren't there. I used to ignore kids. After the perfunctory introductions by the parents at the beginning of the session, the only real contact we would have was if the child were participating in a training exercise. If questions regarding the child needed to be answered, I would ask the parent, even though the child was sitting right there. I am happy to say I have changed my ways.

Talk to kids. You might be thinking, *What do I have to say to a ten-year-old? I have no idea what kids are into!* That's okay; neither do I. So I ask them. Or I might notice something that gives a hint as to what the kid likes or does. Recently, in a client's living room, a Brownies uniform was laid across a chair with a patch nearby. It was a perfect opportunity to engage nine-year-old Kyla. I asked her about Brownies. Was it like Girl Scouts? Was Mom going to sew that patch on her uniform? Did they get different patches? For what? Let kids tell you about their lives. They are usually so thrilled an adult is taking an interest, that you will get a lot more cooperation when you begin the actual training.

There are lots of jumping-off points for questions. Billy might be wearing clothing with a sports team emblazoned on it, or wearing his hair in an unusual style; maybe Danielle, who is very graceful, is taking ballet or gymnastics; perhaps there's a cool toy that's laying around you can ask about. Sometimes the time of year or an upcoming holiday provides a lead-in for conversation. At

Halloween I ask kids what they plan to dress up as. If they are out of school for the summer, how do they feel about that? Are they going to do anything special, maybe take a vacation? Obviously, you don't want to take up a lot of your training time with these conversations, but it is well worth a few minutes of your session to make the child comfortable with you and therefore with the training process.

Training Should Be Fun

Training should be fun for everyone, but especially so for kids. If kids feel something is a chore, they will not want to do it. You will find that some kids have been coerced into being involved in the dog's training. Parents will often say things like, "Justin is twelve. It's his dog, so he'll be doing the training." Does Justin *want* to do the training? Maybe, maybe not. It's likely Justin thought having a dog would entail throwing balls and wrestling, and maybe having the dog sleep in his bed. And why not? He's twelve. Training sounds like work, and Justin is already on the defensive because it's one more thing Mom is making him do.

You will run across kids who are afraid of the dog and therefore apprehensive about training. Others are afraid to try something at which they might fail; and some are simply not interested. The good news is, regardless of the child's initial attitude, it is not difficult to make training enjoyable and by doing so, get the child involved.

Playing games is a great way to alleviate anxiety and pressure; it also makes training fun. One example of a game I love to get kids involved in is the "round-robin recall," where family members take turns calling the dog to them. I encourage kids to be as crazy as they'd like to get the dog to come to them, and to really lavish attention on the dog when he gets there. Once the dog is reliably coming when called by each person, we up the ante by turning it into a game of hide and seek. When it is the child's turn, they run and hide, then call the dog. This game quickly turns reticent children into enthusiastic trainers, and encourages fast, joyful recalls as well.

There is another wonderful game that allows kids to "go wild" while teaching dogs self-control. Although there are different versions of the game, I first heard it described by trainer September Morn. She calls it "Go Wild and Freeze". There is a description of how to play on her web site (http://hometown.aol.com/ morndogs/myhomepage/index.html). In a nutshell, players run around, yelling and flailing their arms. When "Freeze!" is called, everyone stops moving and the dog must instantly sit. Can you imagine how much fun this game is for kids? Every time I have ever played it everyone, including the adults, has laughed and had a great time. Who'd have thought, a teacher who gives kids permission to be wacky and out of control. Kids love this stuff! And if the "homework" is to play these games with their friends, you can bet kids are going to follow through.

When I taught group classes, I noticed a strange phenomenon. When my students trained obedience exercises like "sit" and "stay," their demeanor was serious and sometimes intense. When they trained their dogs to do tricks, they lightened up, smiled and even laughed. Tricks are fun! For that reason, I try to have children teach the dog at least one trick. It can be as simple as having the dog give a paw or target a hand (where the dog touches his nose to the child's hand). For more difficult tricks, you can train the trick and then have the child practice giving the dog the cue and rewarding him. Pretty soon, the child can show the trick off to friends. Pretty cool stuff!

Training for Tots

Even younger kids can get involved in training. This can be especially helpful for kids who are overwhelmed by the dog or a little bit scared of him. Safe, easy exercises that give kids a feeling of control are best. For example, to teach a puppy to lick hands instead of nipping them, teach "Kisses". This is accomplished by smearing a bit of peanut butter on the back of the hand; then, as the pup licks, say, "Kisses". Kids love this. You model it first, then have them do it. There is something so funny to kids about putting peanut butter on the back of their hands (and I'm always making silly comments about peanut butter perfume and such). Even a four-year-old can do this. Of course, parents are shown how to supervise.

Another way to get kids of any age involved in training is to have them act as distractions. I have a client whose eleven-year-old daughter is a budding gymnast. We have her do cartwheels across the living room carpet while Buster does his down-stays. Trainer Donna Duford recommends what she calls "structured silliness." She gives kids very specific instructions, i.e. to run from point A to point B while yelling, "Geronimo!" She adds an element of gaming by having the child begin on her count of "One, two, three, go!" In my experience, kids love this approach!

Begin with small distractions and build up slowly. For example, first, have the child walk by slowly, then pick up the pace a bit. Next, raise the bar to waving arms while walking, gradually building toward clapping hands, doing jumping-jacks, turning cartwheels, running, screaming, or whatever else you or the child can come up with. Encourage kids to be creative and help to think of ideas, the sillier the better. The kid gets to show off and have fun and the dog gets useful, real-life training.

Even kids who are too uncomfortable or too young to do actual training can get involved. Maybe they can help stick gold stars on the dog's progress chart. Or, have them create a Doggie Dictionary. Get parents to start them off by writing the name of a different behavior on each page, i.e. Sit or Down. The child can then draw a picture of the dog doing that behavior. Even doing a simple thing like this will make the child feel involved.

Speaking Kid-ese

Though we do not want to talk down to kids, it is important to talk to them on a level they understand. While I might instruct a fourteen-year-old to stand still, fold her arms and look away when the dog jumps, for an five-year-old, I'll call the action, "Be a tree". (A trainer friend calls this "Freeze like a popsicle!") Do not expect very young kids to be able to carry out instructions reliably. For them, it is more a matter of parental supervision and management. You can, however, make rules for young kids that are safe and easy to follow. I might tell a five-year-old, "The rule is, when you're going to pet the dog, she's got to have a toy in her mouth first." Of course, parents must enforce these rules.

Use analogies with kids that are understandable and relate to their lives. For example, when explaining it is better to train the dog in four short sessions a day rather than one long one, I might ask the child whether he would like to sit in a classroom for two hours straight. Of course he wouldn't, and neither would Fido.

Demonstrations are also useful to clarify a concept. When I explain that many dogs do not like to be patted with a flat palm over the head, I have the child pretend to be the dog. I ask what kind of dog he or she would like to be. A Beagle? "Okay, Buddy the Beagle, I'm going to say hello to you in two different ways. You tell me which you like better." First, I approach slowly, calmly stroke the child's cheek with the side of my palm, and say hello in a soft voice. For the second illustration, I approach brusquely, fingers spread and palm facing down, and pat the child's head repeatedly as I loudly bellow, "Hello!" I make sure the palm is coming down at a bit of an angle from above and in front so the "dog" gets the full effect of that huge hand coming toward him. Almost all kids will say the first approach was nicer. You can then agree and say the dog thinks so too.

Training Tips

Be sure you are the one who shows the child what to do, rather than you showing the parents and having them show the child. After all, it is not as helpful to learn from someone who just learned a technique as it is to learn directly from the expert. And again, kids might accept instructions better from you, the professional, than from their parents.

It is especially important to break things down into small pieces for kids. They need to experience early success so they feel good about training and want to continue. Make sure the dog has been "warmed up" on an exercise with you first before handing him over to the child. If the exercise is one the dog is just learning, be sure you have done plenty of repetitions so that if the child gives the signal or lure slightly differently, the dog will make that mental leap and go with it.

Take the pressure off kids. For some exercises, have the child practice the motions without the dog present. For example, even a hand signal can be difficult for children to do correctly with the dog standing in front of them. So put Rex in another room and have Cindy practice making the signal for Sit a few times. Then

95

bring Rex back out and coach Cindy through it. If Bobby is having trouble luring Rex to lie down, don't keep repeating the instructions. Instead, put your hand over Bobby's and gently guide him through the correct motion a few times. He'll get it. Do not expect kids to do things like walk the dog on leash while clicking and treating. Assign at task suitable for the child's age and coordination level. It could be to deliver the treat, or simply to click on time, followed by the parent delivering the treat.

Kids can have faster reflexes and better timing than adults. For that reason, getting kids involved in clicker training is an excellent idea. Just be sure parents know not to leave clickers around very young children who are likely to treat them as toys. If you are not familiar with clicker training, Peggy Tillman's book *Clicking with Your Dog* is a clear, simple resource to start with and has plenty of exercises kids can do. Kids love it when I tell them, "Wow, you did that even better than your Mom!" And they definitely get a kick out of, "Make sure your parents do their homework!"

Keep in mind that kids can be very sensitive. Offer lots of verbal reinforcement and coach parents to do the same. Be sure that any feedback they give their kids is phrased in a positive way. It is important for the kids to feel a sense of accomplishment. If I have parents who constantly berate their child for doing things incorrectly, I will privately review with them how to phrase things in a more positive manner. I will also, of course, be modeling that phrasing myself throughout the lesson. It is possible when the parents see how well the child responds to my praise and encouragement, they will make an effort to give more of it.

Remember the part about treating your clients like dogs? Treat kids like puppies. Don't expect them to get things right away. Realize that kids, like puppies, have very short attention spans.

Break up rounds of practicing an exercise with other things. Let the kids run in the house and watch television while you continue to work with the parents outdoors, or do something else while you are talking to the parents about that "boring behavior stuff". Realize that kids, like pups, may be out of control and not very well behaved. Be patient, give lots of positive reinforcement, and keep them involved so that training is fun for the whole family.

"There are two ways of meeting difficulties:
you alter the difficulties
or you alter yourself meeting them."

— Phyllis Bottome

Sticky Situations

There are some situations that can throw even the most experienced trainers. These "clashes with clients" can make us feel uncomfortable or angry, or leave us totally baffled as to how to respond. Some scenarios occur with enough regularity that I felt they deserved a section of their own.

Unrealistic Expectations

I had a hard time with this one when I first started doing in-home training. Picture this: Laura and Brad, owners of six-month-old Max the Lab, tell you they would like Max to hang out with them on the front lawn of their suburban home. You reply that sounds like a great way for Max to get socialization. They then clarify that Max would be off-leash and expected to stay on the small, unfenced square of grass. After all, Joe down the street has a dog who is left loose on the front lawn but never tries to leave. So what's wrong with this picture? Well, Joe's dog is a twelve-year-old Basset Hound, and Laura and Brad have unrealistic expectations.

Personally, I do not teach off-leash boundary training in busy suburban or urban areas, because I don't believe it is ever 100% safe. (And even if I did, I would never expect a six month old puppy to be reliable.) Years ago, I had trouble putting my foot down with clients. Now I explain that no matter how well trained the dog, there will always be that stray cat, other dog or distraction across the road, which can be a very bad thing when presented in combination with an oncoming vehicle. Regardless of what the client's unrealistic expectation involves, it is your job is to state politely but firmly that it is not going to happen. If you are having

99

a difficult time of it, hang in there. With experience comes confidence. It gets easier.

Clouded Perceptions

Closely related to unrealistic expectations, clouded perceptions involve the client not seeing the dog's behavior clearly. This can take many forms. Some clients are convinced their dog is "just plain bad" or "stubborn". They cannot get the dog to listen to them, so it must be "defiant". (This particular form of clouded perception also includes being anthropomorphic.) Others have rescued dogs and attribute everything the dog does to having been "abused". The fact is, plenty of rescued dogs were never abused; mostly, they were neglected and/or poorly socialized. But the kind person who took the dog in is now overly lax with the "poor thing," so the training is lax as well.

Whatever the clouded perception, you can certainly give a brief explanation of what the reality is—but talk alone is not likely to change the person's mind. It will not help to simply say, "Sarah, it's unlikely that Shadow has been hit and that's why he won't come when you call." Show, don't tell. Once you get Shadow running joyfully to you when called, it will be hard for Sarah to argue that he can not do it. Once the "stubborn" dog is doing better, it will become apparent the dog is not so stubborn after all. Be sure clients see the dog's success, and shape them gradually away from clouded perceptions.

If the perception is harmless and makes the owner feel better, you might want to keep quiet. While it is important to correct the perception that four-month-old Zara is nippy rather than aggressive, letting Rosie believe that Jax loves her more than he does her husband (despite indications to the contrary) is harmless.

Better Late Than Never?

There will be latecomers in almost any group class. When I began teaching classes, if the class started at 7:00 p.m. and only five of seven students were present, I would wait another ten minutes for the last two to show. All that did was teach stragglers it was no big deal to show up late, as the nice instructor would wait and you wouldn't have missed a thing. Start your classes on time even if there is only one person there. Once everyone is present, make a big deal of thanking and rewarding those who showed up on time. Your ratio of on-time students to late ones will improve. Play a fun game at the beginning of class. Oh, too bad, the latecomers didn't get to play—and it looked like everyone was having so much fun. Darn, there were even prizes! Just as we do with dogs, ignore behavior you do not want and reward the heck out of behavior you do want.

Emotional Blackmail

Ooh. I hate this one! So does every trainer I know. You get a call from a person who sounds extremely distressed. There has been a horrendous problem with the dog for quite some time. Now the owner is at the end of the proverbial rope. "If you don't fix this dog," the caller threatens, "it's going back to the shelter tomorrow." This person, who has not done a thing to "fix the dog" all this time, is now demanding that you, a total stranger, take responsibility for turning the dog around. And not only that, the ultimatum specifies, you must do it right away—*or else*. This one really used to get me, and can still leave me with a bad feeling for days. Having come from a background of doing rescue work, my Inner Rescuer wants to spring forth and shout, "Hang on! I'll save you!"

It's Not the Dogs, It's the People!

No matter how badly you might feel, do not get sucked into the drama. Remain calm and steer the conversation away from the emotional outpouring, to the facts. Determine whether the problem can be easily resolved. If it can, by all means, tell the caller he is in luck and go for it. (At the appointment, you might mention it is a good idea to address problems when they first arise, not months later.) If it is not possible to fix the problem quickly, say so, even if you fear the dog really might lose its home. As much as the situation might tug at your heartstrings, downplaying the problem or saying you can solve it quickly when you can't, would be unethical.

People say all kinds of things when they are frustrated and upset. Just remember, this is emotional blackmail. The more you remain neutral and simply deal with the facts, the better chance the dog has of staying in its home and the better chance you have of staying emotionally balanced so you can go on to train another day. Do what you can but don't let owners make you feel responsible for their problems.

Soft Clients and Hard Reality

It is always heartwarming to see clients treat their dogs well. However, some clients spoil their dogs to such an extent that it undermines what you are trying to accomplish. You, of course, can get the soft client's dog to do just about anything. Ask the client to get Fifi to sit, however, and you hear, "Sit, sit, come on Fifi, sit pleeease!" When trying to get a soft client to follow a leadership program, you are apt to be met with: "What do you mean, she has to do something to *earn* her food? This is my *baby*!" While it can be difficult to make soft clients see things clearly and change their ways, it is critical to success.

Nowhere is it more crucial to instill a realistic perspective than in a case where aggression is involved. Very often the soft client is the one who has been bitten. The dog might not have delivered a severe bite yet, but if things don't change, it could happen. Sometimes it is necessary to paint a grim picture to make the soft client see the gravity of the situation. If she does not follow your advice, you might explain, things will soon be a lot worse for poor Fifi, as rehoming is not an option for aggressive dogs and Fifi could end up having to be euthanised.

Don't pull the rug out from under soft clients by expecting them to change everything at once. Work with them to find realistic solutions. Offer reassurance that they will still be able to love and treat their dog well and that their dog will still love them. In fact, the relationship will actually improve. If you can get the soft client to buy in to what you are saying, to visualize the relationship as different but still loving and to change things in small increments, your program will be successful.

I Guarantee It

Every now and then a prospective client will ask, "What sort of guarantee do you offer?" While some trainers allow students to repeat group classes gratis, most private trainers do not offer a guarantee. Reasons vary from trainer to trainer. As one who only does in-home training, here is my rationale for not offering a guarantee: one, a dog is not a sweater; it is a living being. How can I guarantee that Bodie, who has bitten five people, will never do it again? Or that Crystal will never again soil the living room carpet as long as she lives? Regardless of how good a job I do training the dog, I can not guarantee the behavior of another living being. That brings us to the second point. I can not guarantee the behavior of the owner! How can I guarantee Skippy will stop jumping on people if teenage son Brad constantly encourages it? How can I guarantee the family will work with Poopsy instead of expecting her to become trained with no effort? I politely explain why I do not offer guarantees. Almost everyone has understood. The few who did not were informed they were free to go elsewhere. Frankly, I suspect I wasn't missing out by not having them as clients.

Mistreating the Dog

A scenario where an owner is mistreating a dog is particularly difficult for most trainers on an emotional level. After all, we are dog lovers. This is one of those situations where what you want to say will hopefully differ from what you actually say. Following is a brief illustration of how *not* to handle a mistreatment situation.

As a volunteer at a Los Angeles city shelter in the early 90s, I was instructed to be helpful to the public, never to argue with people relinquishing dogs, and certainly never to chastise them. As you can imagine, this was challenging at times. I dutifully followed the rules, right up until the day a man came in to relinquish his Jindo. The dog refused to walk in the front door. The man tried dragging him, to no avail. He then hauled off and smacked the dog repeatedly. As luck would have it, no other volunteers or staff were present. I was mortified. I finally walked up and told the man in no uncertain terms that the next thing he did to that dog, I was going to do to him. I'm sure he thought I was crazy and possibly dangerous. He stopped smacking the dog immediately.

I almost got fired. I had let my emotions get the better of me. The moral is, "Never put a volatile redhead in a volatile situation." No, wait, that's not it. The moral is, whether we witness or suspect mistreatment in a training situation, we must keep our emotions in check.

When someone in your group class handles his or her dog roughly, or is actually abusive, try to remain calm. Do not confront or threaten. Instead, try to ascertain what the problem is and find a better solution. For example, Colleen is trying to get Moose to sit. Moose won't do it. Colleen keeps pushing down on Moose's rear, which only makes him more determined to stand up. Colleen's fuse is getting shorter and she smacks Moose on the rear, hard. Though you want to run over and say, "Don't hit him!" Colleen (and Moose) will be better served by a low-key approach. Smile as you smoothly insert yourself between Moose and Colleen and ask to take Moose's leash. Then say, "Let me show you an easier way to do that," and show Colleen how luring with a food treat makes sit happen. Get Moose to do the exercise successfully a few times with you so he will be more likely to do it the next time Colleen tries it. Be sure you see Colleen and Moose through a few successful repetitions of the exercise.

Do what you can to influence the way students treat their dogs. However, if you are certain someone is actually abusing a dog, do not hesitate to report that person to the proper authorities.

Let's Make a Deal

Some people live their lives feeling they have not gotten the best deal if they don't negotiate. Haggling may be their normal mode of operation in business transactions and personal relationships. Don't let it apply to you. When a negotiator calls, he will want to "discuss" things. *Hmm, your rates are a bit high. Couldn't you come down, say, ten dollars? And that 9:00 a.m. appointment is a tad early. That's usually breakfast time. Could we meet at 10:00*

105

instead? Rest assured, if you give in to the negotiator at the start, you will be dealing with continued attempts to haggle over every little thing. *Do we really have to walk the dog twice a day? Why must the dog be on leash when guests arrive? It's such a hassle to go get the leash each time.*

Don't go there. Put your foot down at the beginning. Your phone conversation sets the tone for the rest of your training relationship. Remember, *you* are the expert, which is why the person is coming to you in the first place. If the negotiator refuses to abide by your rules, let him go elsewhere. It is hard enough to motivate people to follow through with training. You don't need someone who questions every little thing from the get-go.

Hot Topics

There are certain things we humans are opinionated and even passionate about, some of which are best avoided as topics of conversation in training sessions. Politics and religion come immediately to mind. If either of those, or another controversial topic comes up, answer politely, "I'd prefer not to discuss that" and steer the conversation back to the task at hand. People have strong beliefs about politics and religion, and establishing that yours are different is not going to help. Remember, people are more likely to cooperate when they feel a certain bond, a sameness. Even if you do have the same beliefs, don't go there. While it is fine to have brief conversations about things that are off-topic, stay away from the hot ones.

TWI: Training While Intoxicated

If you do group classes long enough, it is likely that someone will eventually show up under the influence of drugs or alcohol.

This can be a touchy situation. You can't just announce in front of the class, "Why, Bob's drunk!" Approach Bob privately. Tell him it seems he is not feeling well and perhaps he should skip this class and go home. If he is only mildly intoxicated, he might go along with the suggestion with minimal fuss. If you are concerned about his ability to drive, ask whether there is someone he would like you to call to pick him up. Do not allow an intoxicated person to put you or your students at risk. If Bob is seriously intoxicated and becomes dangerously disruptive or belligerent, tell him privately he must settle down or leave, or you arc going to call the police. Follow through if necessary.

"I Have a Friend..."

A caller says she has a neighbor who is having a problem with his dog. This well-meaning guy, she explains, can not get his dog to stop darting out the front door. He has kids who leave the door open and little Shotzie keeps running into the street. It has gotten out of hand, and he and his wife need help. So why, you inquire, aren't these people calling you themselves? Well, you see, the wife is so busy taking the kids to cheerleading practice and softball games, and he works long hours, so she thought she would help by calling around for them. Couldn't you please just give them a call?

Don't do it. I used to, and here is what I found: If these well-meaning people are not even motivated enough to pick up the phone to call you themselves, they are not going to be motivated to follow through with any suggestions you make. Even if another trainer or former client is the one offering the phone number of a prospective client, thank them and explain why you would prefer the person call you instead. In my experience, most people understand and will pass your number along. You will save

107

yourself a lot of grief in the long run by insisting that people make the effort to call you themselves.

"Something Has Come Up..."

When you do private training sessions, you expect to deal with a certain amount of rescheduling and cancellations. Life happens. Illness, family emergencies and other legitimate reasons for cancelling come up. Where you draw the line for acceptable excuses is up to you. Suppose Brenda calls to cancel an appointment. She says she has had an extremely busy week at work and just hasn't had time to work with Muffin. Personally, if I have worked with Brenda a few times and like her, and she normally does her homework and keeps her appointments, I have no problem rescheduling. That's assuming she gave a fair amount of notice. After all, a person knows before the last minute whether there has been time to work with the dog during the week. (And you could certainly point out that in the future, more notice would be better.) If you decide to accept an excuse and reschedule, no matter how annoyed you are, be pleasant about it.

How you handle cancellations financially depends on your sales structure. If you sell blocks of sessions the point might be moot, since the client has already paid for the sessions ahead of time. In that case, all you have to do is remind the client the contract stipulates the entire course of sessions must be completed within a certain amount of time. Whether you sell packages of sessions or not, you should have a clause in your training contract about cancellations. Most trainers stipulate if clients cancel with less than twenty-four hours notice they must pay for the session, or at least pay a minimal cancellation fee.

I do not insist on people buying packages, and I try to be flexible regarding scheduling, up to a point. What I do *not* want is to be perpetually stuck with last-minute cancellations, especially when I could have had other appointments in their place. How strictly you enforce policy is up to you, but if it is in your contract that cancelled appointments are billable, gently remind the client of that point and proceed from there.

Clients who constantly cancel appointments are a different story. It is one thing for a client to cancel because her child has the flu, then the next week because she's caught it. That's legitimate in my book and frankly, I would rather not catch it myself and miss weeks of work. I will duly note on the client's information sheet when and why the cancellation occurred for future reference.

If a client gives a "too busy" or other not-quite-legitimate excuse more than once or twice, I will drop that client. I will refer to my client sheet and remind her of previous appointments she has cancelled and explain that I cannot run my business that way. I will suggest she might be better off working with another trainer. No matter how angry you are about a cancellation, whether it is because the client has done so twice before or is canceling an hour before your appointment, be polite and deal with it as neutrally as possible. Then hang up and vent.

You might have noticed that many of the solutions to "sticky situations" involve keeping your cool and being unfailingly polite. There is something to be said for *not* voicing what you want to at all times, and not getting defensive. Even when you feel your next session with a client should be scheduled for, say, when hell freezes over, tell them so calmly and not in those words. Regardless of the situation, maintain a calm tone of voice and phrase things in ways that will encourage compliance rather than cause defenses to rise. Above all, always be professional.

"Early and provident fear is the mother of safety."

- Edmund Burke

Personal Safety

You might find it strange that a book geared toward working with people would include a chapter on how to protect yourself *from* them. The fact is, the majority of professional dog trainers are female. The majority of victims of personal assaults, particularly sexual, are also female.

If you are a male trainer you might prefer to skip this section. But regardless of your gender, you never know when you might find yourself in an unsafe situation. So although it might be a bit off-topic, I hope you will read this section and take it to heart. Who knows, the information might some day help you to avoid a dangerous situation or be able to extract yourself from one safely. This section is not geared so much toward those who do group classes, but more so, to those who do private, in-home training. While a student might be drunk, belligerent or even threatening in a group class, the stakes are much higher when you are alone in someone's home.

My Wake-Up Call

I like to think I can take care of myself. I grew up in New York City, where you learn at an early age to be aware of your surroundings. You also develop a kind of radar about people, and a certain toughness. That said, I want to share a story that took place in Southern California, where I live now. It does not end in anything quite so dramatic as my getting assaulted; but the experience was definitely a wake-up call.

One day last summer, a man phoned and said he wanted his Dalmatian mix to stop darting out the front door. He sounded a

111

bit…odd. I couldn't quite put my finger on it. As all his answers to my many questions seemed appropriate, despite my uneasy feeling, we set up an appointment. "Lucas, not Luke or Lou" lived further out in the desert than my usual travel range. His home, which was at least a mile from any other homes or businesses, consisted of a trailer with a chain link fence around it. I got out of my Jeep and was greeted by a large, stocky man with wild, dirty hair and grease under his nails. Since there were a few cars and tractors in his front "yard" that were in various states of repair, it seemed logical he might be a mechanic, which would at least partially explain his appearance. I followed him inside where, much to my relief, sat an adorable Dalmatian mix.

Lucas sprawled in a chair while I stood in his small living room, nervously rambling on. I did not like the way he was looking at me, and I got the distinct impression he was not entirely focused on what I was saying. As I spoke, I scanned the room. To my right, hanging on the wall, was the biggest shotgun I have ever seen. It gave me a jolt. I instantly rationalized it as acceptable, however, since many people in rural areas keep shotguns. When I saw the second shotgun hanging on the other wall, I told myself he probably likes shotguns so much he collects them. But I was getting nervous, and experiencing the most unpleasant reality check about my personal safety. I kept thinking maybe I was just being paranoid, but my gut disagreed.

At this point I must interject a bit of personal information so you understand what happened next. An ex-boyfriend (who coincidentally had the same unusual name as this man, with the same abhorrence of nicknames), turned out to be one of the most dangerous people I have ever met. We are talking about a man who stalked me when I tried to leave him; and, he collected martial arts weapons and guns. So when a few moments later I noticed a

Samurai sword lying on the floor, it stopped me cold. I stopped dead in the middle of a sentence and blurted, "I see you have a Samurai sword. Do you collect that sort of thing?" His face lit up. "Actually," he offered, "I collect all sorts of weapons. Would you like to know what my favorite is?" Being the perverse person I am, I answered yes. "Machine guns!" he answered gleefully, followed by, "Would you like to come in the back and see some?" I respectfully declined. Not only are machine guns illegal to own in the state I live in (unless you are a licensed dealer, which I'm guessing he wasn't), but there was something decidedly creepy about the whole thing. Red flags were unfurling in my mind.

There was more, including a lone baby stroller I spotted out back, despite the fact that he had told me he had no wife or children (which he reiterated while shaking his head sadly). When I asked why he had a baby stroller, he explained that a student who lived nearby came to clean his house weekly and brought her child with her. (I don't know too many people who live in trailers that have cleaning people, do you?) Why this girl would leave a stroller behind is beyond me, but as you might have fathomed, at that point I was ready to jump at the slightest provocation. I was imagining what, or who, was buried in that back yard! Somehow I managed to keep my cool and get through the appointment, and when he suggested we set up another session for the following week I agreed, to avoid any confrontation. I just wanted out. I'd worry about canceling the appointment later.

The next day I left a message on Lucas' answering machine saying I hadn't realized he lived so far away, and that it would not be possible to continue our training. I provided him with the name of a male trainer in his area. He phoned me back a week later. He wanted to know why I hadn't shown up for our appointment. His voice sounded strained and angry. I said I had left him a message,

113

to which he replied that he had not received any messages. As neutrally as possible, I repeated what the message had said. He then demanded, "Are you sure there's not some other reason you don't want to work with me?" When I feigned ignorance he said in an accusatory tone, "You seemed a little freaked out by the weapons."

Yes, friends, I certainly had been "freaked out". And now I was feeling certain I had been right about Lucas. His tone was angry out of proportion to the situation, and I knew in my heart he really had gotten the phone message and was lying to perpetuate contact. Something was definitely not right.

Listen to Your Instincts

I believe in listening to your instincts. I never should have gone to Lucas' house in the first place. In retrospect, nothing untoward happened, at least on the surface. There was no grabbing, no assault, not even a verbal suggestion of one. But something was definitely not right. I might have been in serious danger.

Gavin de Becker is a personal safety specialist. His agency provides protection and support to celebrities and others who are being stalked or otherwise threatened, as well as working with government agencies on security matters. The most important piece of advice de Becker gives in his excellent book *The Gift of Fear* (see *Resources*) is to *listen to your instincts*. He makes a case for the fact that what we normally think of as "intuition" is really the subconscious picking up minute details and sending up warning flags. He deems intuition "soaring flight as compared to the plodding of logic." You would think as professionals who pride ourselves on being able to predict a dog's behavior, we would listen to our instincts more on predicting human behavior.

114

Phone Screening

I am not suggesting female trainers become paranoid every time a man calls for help with his dog. I have plenty of male clients who never gave me a moment of pause over the phone or in person. But if someone does cause you to feel apprehensive, ask a lot of questions. Some of these are questions you would probably ask anyway, but what we are looking for here is specific details in the answers.

Where did you get the dog?
I am always relieved to hear the name of a specific rescue group, shelter or breeder with whom I am familiar. "Some pet store, I can't remember the name" does not make me feel as safe.

What are the dog's issues?
A detailed description such as, "My kids sometimes leave the table during dinner, and last week Duke grabbed a piece of meat from Kimmy's dish" puts me more at ease than, "Well, you know, he just needs training."

How were you referred?
In the best of all worlds, the caller would name a previous client as the referral source. But if you get referrals from vets, groomers and other businesses as well, it might not be that easy. Try to get a specific answer. I want to hear, "Dr. Anderson referred me" rather than "I got a flyer from a vet's office, I can't remember which one." If he has a dog, unless it's a brand new adoption, he should be able to name his vet, or ask his wife for the name.

If you have magnetic car signs on your vehicle, the answer to how he found you might be that he has "seen you driving around". If your brochure or web site includes photos of you, perhaps he saw those. None of those answers engenders a warm, fuzzy feeling in me. And by the way, if you are a self-admitted "psycho magnet" like me, you might want to consider modifying your advertising. When Lucas, the machine-gun-collecting desert dude, said he had seen me driving around town numerous times, I removed my magnetic car signs immediately. It just creeped me out to think of him noticing me around town; and he still lives here. Of course, for most trainers, the signs never would have been a problem, and they're good for business.

Who else lives in the home?
Plenty of nice guys live alone. However, if there is something off-putting about someone on the phone to begin with, I am always relieved to hear there is a wife and kids. And, suspicious person that I am, I want to know they really exist. I might ask open-ended questions such as, "How does your wife feel about Max jumping on visitors?" or "Why did you and your wife decide Max needs training right now?" If he goes into a believable, specific answer, all the better.

Of course, you can ask endless questions and someone who is intelligent and has been around dogs long enough could manufacture some pretty specific, detailed answers. But a careful screening process, along with listening to your gut feeling, should provide some measure of safety.

Preventive Measures

If you are going to do a private, in-home session, it is important to let someone know where you will be. I have a dry-erase board where I note for my husband the name, address and phone number of the client I am going to see. I would like to tell you I do this for every appointment, but the truth is, I don't. I probably should, and if you live with someone, so should you. If it is a female client I have no reservations about (which is the norm), I don't bother. If it is a male client, regardless of whether I have reservations or not, I leave the information.

Carry a cell phone. Be sure the batteries are charged and you have a pre-set 911 button. Most cell phones come with the preset—be sure yours does, or set it yourself. Everyone thinks it would be no big deal to dial three little numbers in an emergency, but trust me, it is. When a guy in a truck hit and almost ran me off a narrow, curving road last year, I tried to call the police as I chased him. (Okay, so my fight or flight response is a bit skewed.) I couldn't manage it, and it wasn't just because I was driving at the time. If someone is threatening you, you might only have seconds to call for help. When you are in a panic and trying to punch numbers on a phone, you feel like you have twenty fingers—and they're all fat.

In a group class, keeping a cell phone with you is important. It is common sense, for dealing with emergencies such as a dog needing medical care. As for your personal safety, even though there are other people present at a group class, there might be a student who is actually dangerous. The person could be intoxicated or mentally unbalanced. Or there might be dangerous people who are not your students but are hanging around the area in which you teach. Either way, it is best to be prepared.

One Carry-On Item, Please

Some trainers carry pepper spray or Direct Stop (a citronella spray in a cannister that resembles pepper spray), as a defense against aggressive canines *or* humans. I have one trainer friend whose key chain has a long, blunt piece of metal attached that could be used for self-defense. But even if you choose to carry something with you, don't be lulled into a false sense of security and take unnecessary chances. The moment I saw that shotgun hanging on Lucas' wall, I had a pathetic vision of trying to spray him with Direct Stop as he aimed the shotgun at my head. ...The best weapon you have is your intuition.

On Location

So what if you get to the home and the aforementioned wife and kids are not present? Maybe the kids really did have a last-minute soccer practice and the wife had to drive them. Not a reason in and of itself to panic, but combined with a certain dis-ease you felt on the phone, a red flag has started waving at the back of your mind. Or perhaps you are home alone with a male client who makes inappropriate personal comments, or brushes against you in a way that's not entirely necessary. The dog has better manners than he does, and you feel one of them has ulterior motives. *These are warning signals.* Be alert and make sure you know where the possible exits are in case you have to make a hasty retreat.

Then there is the obvious, in-your-face inappropriate behavior. Here is what happened to a good friend of mine, a well-known male trainer, back when he was working as a wallpaper hanger: He had gone to a man's home for a consultation. The man was behaving nervously during the appointment, at one point moving quickly to close a bedroom door before my friend could see inside. When it came time to sit down and choose colors, the man leaned over and placed his finger on my friend's jeans, two inches from his crotch, and said pointedly, "I want *that* color." My friend, to his credit, was direct and professional. He stood up and said, "You need to find another contractor to work with."

118

If you find yourself in an obvious situation such as this, the appropriate response is to tell the client you feel he would be better off with another trainer, or that you simply don't feel comfortable working with him. Many women find it difficult to to come right out and say something that direct. We have, after all, been conditioned by society to be polite and not make waves. But consider this: in de Becker's book, he cites case after case where women were raped, assaulted and otherwise violated because during their initial exchange with the attacker, they did not want to be impolite. Sound silly? We do it all the time.

In one case, a man approached a woman who was on her way to her apartment and asked if he could help with her groceries. The woman repeatedly declined but the man persisted, finally saying, "There's such a thing as being *too* proud, you know." The woman finally gave in. As de Becker puts it, "This seemingly insignificant exchange between the cordial stranger and the recipient of his courtesy was the signal—to him and to her—that she was willing to trust him. As the bag passed from her control to his, so did she."

De Becker says, "Safety is the preeminent concern of all creatures and it clearly justifies a seemingly abrupt and rejecting response from time to time". And he's right. But if you feel you might be risking confrontation or escalating the situation by being direct, here are some alternatives:

Carry a pager in your pocket. Pagers are often set to vibrate rather than beep, especially during meetings. So it wouldn't be unusual for you to look startled, reach into your pocket, pull out your pager and say, "I'm so sorry, I have a 911 page and my sister is in the hospital. I need to leave right away. I'll call you later to reschedule."

119

Another tactic is to suddenly realize there is some training tool that would be helpful for the task at hand, but it happens to be in your car. "You know, a head halter would really help Daisy. I have some in the car. I'll be right back." Once you are in the car—floor it. Of course, you will likely get a call asking why you left. At that point you can tell the truth, but I try not to create unnecessary conflict. You could say that once you got in the car your cell phone had a message and it was an emergency.

You could follow up by saying you have since realized that: a) the person lives too far away and all your clients are on the other side of town; or b) you really don't feel you are the best trainer for the situation because (insert excuse here); or c) your schedule is so full that you are not going to be able to reschedule for a long while. It really doesn't matter what you say, as long as you disengage from the person without creating conflict.

Worst Case Scenario

If the worst happens and it is no longer possible to get out of the situation, do what you must to defend yourself. It would be impossible to offer specific advice here, as each situation is different and everyone has a different response. But it is not a bad idea to take a self-defense class to get a few techniques under your belt.

I realize that after reading all this, you might think my attitude overly cautious. Perhaps it is. I have not heard of a single case of a trainer being lured to someone's home and being attacked. Thank goodness, most people out there really do just want Buddy to stop jumping on visitors, and are not trying to get you alone. But when you perform a service which necessitates spending time in people's homes, it would be foolish not to consider these things.

Perhaps this chapter will serve as your wakeup call, and help you avoid one like I had. Always remember: Above all else, follow your instincts.

"If a man insisted always on being serious, and never allowed himself a bit of fun and relaxation, he would go mad or become unstable without knowing it."

- Herodotus

"There is no need to go to India or anywhere else to find peace. You will find that deep place of silence right in your room, your garden or even your bathtub."

- Elisabeth Kubler-Ross

"Take it easy."

- The Eagles

Taking Care of Dog's Best Friend

When you are doing something you love, your energy level soars. The outside world fades away as you become blissfully immersed. You are in "The Zone". I feel that way about a great training session. Even if I have begun in a foul state of mind, making progress with a lovely dog and owner turns it all around. I hope training does the same for you.

That said, all of us have off days. We can be moody; have trouble concentrating; can't remember things; or we don't feel well. Let's face it, some days we are just not at the top of our game. At those times, we might not be as pleasant or helpful with clients as we'd like. We might even wish appointments would cancel. Sometimes it's just "one of those days". But if you find yourself having those days more and more often, or you are becoming impatient, irritable or callous to your clients, take a step back and take stock.

What's the Problem?

Assess the problem as you would a behavior issue. Where does the problem lie? What needs to be modified? Perhaps you have been working too many hours and it is time for a vacation. Maybe there are issues in your life that need to be dealt with, or you need to get more sleep or exercise. Whatever it is, address the problem so you can remain a positive force for your clients and their dogs.

Take the time to relax. (And yes, that's easier said than done!) Relaxation is not only necessary to maintain health, but is an investment in keeping your business successful. After all, one can only go so long being stressed mentally, physically or emotionally before burning out or becoming ill.

It's Not the Dogs, It's the People!

Release Stress and Stay in Balance

It is ironic that while we advocate proper exercise and nutrition for our canine clients, we often forego it ourselves. Rest, exercise and eat well. Being well rested is crucial to performing at the top of your game, and is particularly important the night before a serious behavior case. You do not want to make a judgment call that could potentially mean life or death for a dog, on three hours of sleep. On a less dramatic note, when I have not had enough sleep, I tend to become irritable and impatient. I want to snap at clients for things that normally would not bother me. Knowing that, I make every effort to get enough rest, even if it means going to bed earlier than I would like. If you take naps, be sure to schedule time to take one before an evening appointment if necessary.

Exercise raises endorphin levels and relieves stress. Even twenty minutes of walking or other cardio-vascular activity three times per week can have a positive effect on your overall emotional and physical well-being. Aerobics, weight training, walking, jogging, bicycling, hiking and other physical activities help not only to keep us in shape physically, but to keep our moods on an even keel. Gentle disciplines such as Yoga, Tai Chi and Chi Gong are also wonderful stress reducers. You probably already know all this—but do you actually do it?

Eating well helps keep moods balanced. We all know the basics of good nutrition, whether we actually follow them or not. (Of course, eating chocolate raises seratonin levels, which promotes calm—so there's no need to go crazy and give up the good stuff entirely!) No matter how busy your schedule, be sure to eat small meals or well-balanced snacks throughout the day to keep your blood sugar levels even and your energy up. Many people become lightheaded, cranky, exhausted or all of the above if they are careless about this. Small protein-based snacks such as cheese or a hard-boiled egg can help. Avoid sugary snacks. That immediate rush is not worth the energy dip you will experience later.

Schedule down time. If you have a few heavy training days in a row, whether that means number of appointments or intensity (i.e. back-to-back severe behavior cases), schedule the next day off. Mental exhaustion can be even more draining than physical exhaustion, and again, you do not want to chance making errors in judgment.

Try to take time off regularly, even if it is only one day a week. "Time off" means you do not see clients, do not answer your business phone and do not return calls. If the thought of losing potential clients stresses you, put an outgoing message on your answering machine stating your hours and, for example, that calls received on Saturday after five or on Sunday will be returned Monday after 8 a.m. Sure, business is important. But so is your mental health. If you don't ever rest you are not going to be able to keep working without eventually burning out.

Vacations… you've heard of them. They're those things people without pets and crazy schedules take. Try one. It doesn't have to be so lengthy it will stress you out with worry about how the fur-kids or your business are doing. Take a long weekend. If you can't swing that, get out of town for a day. Take a long drive to an area you don't normally go to—the change of scenery will help.

Even if you can't get away for so much as a day, you can still take short breaks throughout your day. Simply closing your eyes and doing deep breathing exercises will refresh and re-energize.

There are numerous books that describe specific breathing exercises for relaxation or offer brief, refreshing meditations. In his excellent book, *The Dog Whisperer* (see *Resources*), trainer Paul Owens describes two breathing exercises. One is quick and easy and can be done anywhere. The other is geared toward more intense relaxation.

Incorporate stretching exercises into your breaks between clients. Anyone can find two minutes to stretch, and it really re-energizes the body. If you drive from appointment to appointment, relax on the way. Bring along music to listen to that makes you feel good. If you are having a rough day, blow off some steam between appointments by calling a friend to chat. Short stress-relief breaks can make all the difference.

Engage in an activity that is purely for fun and has nothing to do with business. If it is dog-related, that's okay too. Take your dog through an agility class or get involved in freestyle or flyball. Non-dog-related (I know you've heard of it) is even better. Take a dance class; join a local study group; play a sport; do charity work. It doesn't matter, so long as it's fun.

Pamper yourself! Whatever your budget, you can find some way to feel wonderful and relaxed. A trainer friend of mine insists on working a weekly massage into her schedule, no matter how busy she is. Good for her! But pampering need not be expensive, and can even be done at home.

Do whatever relaxes you. Meditate; take a long candle-lit bath; give yourself a facial; read; get into your flannel pajamas with a big bowl of popcorn and watch a great movie. Or hang out with a friend whose company makes you feel good. It doesn't matter what it is, so long as you enjoy it. If you find yourself continually saying, "I just don't have the time," *make* the time. Work the activity into your schedule, write it on your calendar, and honor it as you would a training appointment.

Sure, you can take every appointment that comes your way and schedule yourself into oblivion. You'll end up with lots of money, albeit not much time to enjoy it. You'll also end up with frazzled nerves and possibly compromised physical health. How well do you think you could serve your clients in that condition?

Do yourself and your clients a favor and be good to yourself. You deserve it and so do they. After all, you are dog's best friend.

For other books by Nicole Wilde,

as well as Nicole's seminar DVDs

and Wilde About Dogs blog, visit

www.nicolewilde.com

Resources

Books

Nicole's books can all be found in hard copy or ebook format at
www.nicolewilde.com. Other dog-related books are available
through www.dogwise.com or amazon.com.
Alternate sources are listed where applicable.

Dealing With People You Can't Stand
Dr. Rick Brinkman & Dr. Rick Kirschner
USA: McGraw-Hill, 1994 ISBN 0-07-007838-6

Since Strangling Isn't An Option
Sandra A. Crowe, M.A.
New York: Penguin Putnam, 1999 ISBN 0-399-52540-8

The Gift of Fear
Gavin de Becker
USA: Little, Brown and Company, 1997 ISBN 0-316-23502-4

The Evans Guide for Counseling Dog Owners
(some good info on people skills, ignore the punishment-based
training methods)
Job Michael Evans
New York: Howell, 1985 ISBN 0-87605-660-5

The Other End of the Leash
Leader of the Pack, The Cautious Canine (booklets)
Patricia McConnell, Ph.D.
Dog's Best Friend, Ltd. (may order in bulk)
608-767-2435
www.dogsbestfriendtraining.com

It's Not the Dogs, It's the People!

The Dog Whisperer: A Compassionate, Nonviolent approach to Dog Training
Paul Owens
Holbrook, MA: Adams Media Corp., 1999 ISBN 1-58062-203-8

Taking Care of Puppy Business
Gail Pivar and Leslie Nelson
Illinois: Tails-U-Win!, 1998
(860) 646-5033
www.tailsuwin.com

Games People Play...
Life Beyond Block Heeling
Terry Ryan
WA: Legacy by Mail, 1996
Legacy Canine Behavior and Training
PO Box 3909
Sequim, WA 98382
360-683-1522
Order through www.legacycanine.com (see site for all books)
e-mail blryan@olypen.com

The New Peoplemaking
Virginia Satir
Science and Behavior Books, Inc., 1988 ISBN 0831400706

Clicking with Your Dog
Peggy Tillman
MA: Sunshine Books, Inc., 2000 ISBN 1-890948-05-5

Teaching Dog Obedience Classes (some good info on people skills—ignore the harsh training methods)
Joachim Volhard and Gail Tamases Fisher
New York: Howell, 1986 ISBN 0-87605-765-2

Videos

The following are available through Tawzer Dog Videos at www.tawzerdogvideos.com

Body Language: The Human Non-Verbal Communication
Body language of humans and animals.
Roger Abrantes

People Skills: Teaching So Your Students Will Listen
Handling challenging students in group classes; how to teach, handle and motivate all students.
Donna Duford

Working With Kids
How to motivate kids to be involved with training and how to work with them productively.
Donna Duford

Choosing Your Battles
Priorities in consultations; convincing owners to follow through; learning to discard or at least disguise some of our opinions.
Trish King

A Picture Is Worth 1000 Words
Explaining training principles through demonstrations, analogies and graphics; behavior and motivational training concepts.
Terry Ryan

Dog Training Would Be Perfect If Not For People
New terms and new ways of thinking about common problems; case studies.
Sarah Wilson

It's Not the Dogs, It's the People!

Nothing But the Facts, Ma'am
Taking an effective history; handling clients and difficult situations smoothly.
Sarah Wilson

Web Sites on Human Body Language

The Non-Verbal Dictionary of
Gestures, Signs & Body Language Cues
(Human communication from a scientific point of view)
www.members.aol.com/nonverbal2/diction1.htm

Decoding Body Language
(Text and illustrations on four basic modes of body language in business)
www.johnmole.com/articles18b.htm

Miscellaneous

APDT (Association of Pet Dog Trainers)
www.apdt.com
Web site offers CD-ROMs of recent conferences. There is usually at least one seminar that focuses on dealing with human clients.